CORPORATE CREDIT ANALYSIS

CORPORATE CREDIT ANALYSIS

Brian Coyle

CIB PUBLISHING

FINANCIAL
EDUCATION

CIB Publishing
c/o The Chartered Institute of Bankers
Emmanuel House
4-9 Burgate Lane
Canterbury
Kent
CT1 2XJ
United Kingdom

Telephone: 01227 762600

CIB Publishing publications are published by The Chartered Institute of Bankers, a non-profit making registered educational charity.

The Chartered Institute of Bankers believes that the sources of information upon which the book is based are reliable and has made every effort to ensure the complete accuracy of the text. However, neither CIB, the author nor any contributor can accept any legal responsibility whatsoever for consequences that may arise from errors or omissions or any opinion or advice given.

Typeset by The Foundry
Printed by WBC Book Manufacturers, Bridgend

© Chartered Institute of Bankers 2000

ISBN 0-85297-451-5

Contents

Introduction

Credit analysis is a structured process of investigation and assessment. The role of the credit analyst is to assess and evaluate the potential credit risk with any customer or borrower, and to advise on decisions about granting credit or providing loans or borrowing facilities.

Credit management in companies has much in common with credit management in banks. In both types of organization, a system is required for deciding how much credit can be given in total, and whether credit should be given (and how much) to individual customers or groups of customers, taking into consideration the credit risk (bad debts, loss of liquidity).

For non-bank companies, giving and taking credit is a normal feature of trading operations. Credit must be given to make sales and earn profit. For banks, giving credit (i.e. lending) is a profit-making operation in itself. Gross profit is the interest earned.

Methods of Analysis

Another title in this series, *Measuring Credit Risk*, describes how decisions about giving or taking credit can be reached, and the various methods of analysis that can be used.

Credit assessments can be obtained externally from credit rating agencies or credit reference agencies. Alternatively (or in addition) assessments can be carried out by in-house staff. Bankers with responsibility for lending decisions, for example, must have some expertize in analysis techniques.

In companies, the responsibility for the credit assessment of banks and major trade customers could be given to the finance director, financial controller or corporate treasurer. Decisions about the total amount of trade credit the company should allow could be taken by the board of directors. The routine day-to-day analysis of individual trade customers is likely to be delegated to the credit manager or operational management.

At a strategic or policy level, a company or bank might wish to assess the risk from its credit exposures to customers in specific industries or countries. At a more detailed level, a large part of credit analysis work is the assessment of individual corporate customers. The purpose of this book is to suggest how credit analysis of individual companies can be carried out.

Analytical Skills

A prime focus of corporate credit analysis should be an assessment of the customer's liquidity. A company that has sufficient money is likely to pay what it owes when the payment falls due. Illiquid companies, including profitable companies with inadequate cash flows, are a serious credit risk.

Credit assessment is not an exact science. There is no single item of information, such as a single financial ratio, which shows whether a company is a good credit risk or not. The analyst must assemble a variety of information, both financial and non-financial, to make a well-reasoned assessment of the risk involved in giving credit to the customer. In many cases, different items of information about a company could seem to conflict and point to a different conclusion.

Credit analysis, particularly in banks, has evolved as a structured process to improve credit decisions. Not all decisions will necessarily be good ones, but an organized and systematic approach can help to raise the quality of credit assessment. Techniques such as credit scoring, computer sensitivity models and cash flow analysis can be used.

Much credit analysis involves an investigation of financial statements and reports. This can be a deterrent to non-financial managers. Even a non-financial manager, however, should be able to understand how financial statements are analyzed, what items of information can be extracted and why they could be relevant to credit assessments. It is always necessary to keep asking common sense questions and being aware of *why* particular items of information or financial ratios could be significant. It is not sufficient to know what information is gathered, and how it is used.

Principles of Good Lending

Each item of information used in corporate credit analysis must be of practical value; otherwise it would not be worth collecting. Since the overall aim of the credit analyst is to reach a judgment about giving credit to a customer, the information used by an analyst must be relevant to the principles of good credit management. For banks, these are the principles of good lending.

The principles of good lending for banks can be reduced to a simplified framework, summarized in a useful mnemonic, *Campari* and *Ice*. This mnemonic stands for:

C Character
A Ability
M Means
P Purpose
A Amount
R Repayment
I Insurance

Character – refers to the honesty and integrity of the business and its management. Borrowers are not necessarily reliable or honest, and the lender must look for evidence of good character, if it exists. Frequently, this can be ascertained during an interview. The lender must, however, be sure to make his own assessment and not rely on the decision of an existing lender, or similarly on a key individual in the company – so called name lending.

Ability – relates to the actual ability of the borrower to enter into a contract with the bank, e.g. a loan made to a minor is not a legally enforceable debt. Similarly for a company, it is whether the directors are acting within the authority extended to them in the company's Articles of Incorporation.

Means – relates to the borrower's technical, managerial and financial means. It might also refer to how a company monitors and manages its risks and the suitability of the assets in the company to generate sufficient levels of cash to repay the loan.

Purpose – the purpose of granting credit must be clear and acceptable to the lender. A loan to settle existing debts to suppliers for example could indicate a serious liquidity problem.

Planned growth in the customer's business would constitute an acceptable purpose; however, it will almost inevitably result in a requirement for more credit from suppliers, even when normal trade credit terms are applied. But credit should not be given to support *excessive* business growth. Lending to a company which is expanding having won a new contract may sound reasonable. However, a request from a similar company which has won five new contracts might raise doubts in the mind of the lender, as the company may not have planned for its growth adequately.

Amount – the level of the loan must be consistent with the purpose and be sufficient in amount. The cost of the purchase price of the asset against the equity contribution provided by the borrower should be compared.

Repayment – addresses the borrower's ability to repay, by looking at the source of repayment. The ability to repay is vital and should ideally be demonstrated through projected cash flows rather than on future profit generation. With corporate lending, the primary source of repayment for a loan is normally the activities that the loan will finance. The type of repayment structure should also be addressed, for example, whether the loan is to be repaid on a bullet or amortizing basis.

Insurance – refers to insurance in the sense of *security*, namely a safety net that a bank can fall back on should the loan not be repaid. A lending proposition should not be security led; however, if taken, ideally it should be an adequate margin over the amount of the loan, easy to value, easy to realize and easy to take.

Care should be taken by the lender to establish whether a trade supplier might have a retention of title over goods supplied, should the lender be looking at those goods as security for its borrowing.

and

   I   Interest
   C   Commissions
   E   Extras

Interest – the term "risk reflects reward" is often used by bankers, namely the higher the risk in a transaction, the greater the interest margin levied. A key factor to consider here is the overall interest cost to the customer, which comprises two elements: the underlying cost of funds (which may be fixed at the outset of the loan, or may be variable in line with the underlying cost of funds), plus a margin.

Commissions – these include any other fees, such as a commitment fee for reserving a facility for a customer for a particular period of time.

Extras – refer to the hidden additional costs associated with provision of the loan, e.g. legal fees.

Summary

Corporate credit analysis is carried out on customers by banks, other companies, credit rating agencies and credit reference agencies or bureaux. The purpose of the analysis is the same in each case, to judge the liquidity of the company. This involves a study of the business, its markets and market position, its management and its financial situation.

Corporate Credit Analysis – Areas for Analysis

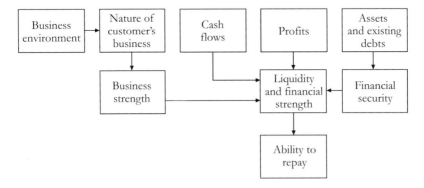

Assessing Companies: The Business Risk

A credit analyst should understand the business of the company that he or she is assessing. There are obvious reasons for wanting this information. The amount of credit or borrowing that the company asks for should be consistent with the size and nature of its business. If the company asks for credit to support business expansion plans, it helps the analyst to know something about the future prospects for the business (growth, decline, the threat from increased competition, the pace of technological change, etc.) and the relative strength of the company within its markets. If a business is in a declining industry, or is trying to expand its operations in a static market, it could eventually have declining profits and a worsening liquidity position. The experience and skills of the company's management, and its technical capacity to deal with anticipated changes in the industry or market, can also be useful indicators of the company's future prospects.

Knowing something about a company's business can also help an analyst to understand more about its financial position; for example why it has a large amount of inventory, why its debts are high, or why its profit margins are low.

The business risk will be much greater for longer-term lending than short-term credit. When a company suffers a downturn in business, or fails to expand as planned, its profitability and liquidity will often decline over time, before reaching the point where the company ultimately cannot pay its debts.

If a company has a short-term liquidity crisis, business risk analysis is unlikely to be of direct practical value. Problems in the company's position will be apparent from financial information. Business risk assessment is therefore more relevant to credit analysis by banks (and by companies wishing to establish a long-term relationship with a supplier) than the assessment of customers for short-term trade credit. When a bank makes a medium-term loan to a company, it is effectively investing in the company's business, and it is naturally sensible for the bank to consider the company's medium-term prospects before it takes the lending decision.

The Company and its Industry

Some understanding of the industry and the markets within which the company operates is fundamental to business risk assessment.

The analyst must know how the company earns its money, i.e. what products or services it sells, where it sells them and at what price. The analyst should also want to know who the major competitors are, and have some idea of the company's share of the market.

Information for analyzing an industry can be obtained externally from industry surveys. Occasional industry surveys are produced by major broking firms, or information may be obtained from publications such as the *Wall St. Journal*. Surveys are also available from specialist companies, such as Dun & Bradstreet.

An analyst can also build up a file of industry information by subscribing to trade magazines, keeping newspaper cuttings or obtaining copies of the annual report and accounts of the leading companies in the industry. Online news retrieval/search services are also available and of course the Internet provides a valuable source of information.

Experience in the industry will be an obvious benefit to the analyst. A credit manager assessing what trade credit terms should be offered to a customer, for example, will often have some direct experience and knowledge of the customer's business.

Management

Rightly or wrongly, a customer's business might be judged according to the impression its management makes. Judgments by lenders and suppliers often without any solid foundation, and boil down to the issue of whether the banker or credit provider personally likes or respects the people involved.

By reputation and tradition, branch managers of retail banks have often been said to base their lending decisions on whether or not they felt that they could trust the customer. The first handshake and the customer's general appearance have probably been decisive factors in lending more often than banks might care to admit.

It is worth mentioning, perhaps, that even in large companies, how a bank views its management can be a significant factor in its decision to continue to support the company.

The quality of management in a company is an important contributor to its success and financial strength. However, judgments about management should be based on more objective reasoning, not just personal impressions and a "feel good" factor. There are a number of objective indicators that can be used. Management ability can be assessed according to the experience, expertise and stability of the senior management team.

The depth of experience of a company's management is not a guarantee in itself against bad debts, but it does provide some indication that the management known their business. In contrast, a lack of experience might suggest that only limited credit should be granted until the management has built up more of a track record.

Stability of the senior management team can also be significant. A history of frequent or wholesale changes at board level would be disconcerting. Even one resignation by a director might raise some doubts about the company, unless the reason for the resignation is satisfactorily explained. The loss of a key person, in particular the chief executive officer or finance director, could be a cause for alarm.

President/Chairman and Chief Executive Officer

In many companies, one or two of the directors are the major stockholders. As such, they are likely to be a dominant influence on company policy and the running of the business. In a significant number of companies the positions of president/chairman and CEO are held by the same person, indicating perhaps that the company is managed in a fairly autocratic way by that one person.

When a company does not have one-man rule, or a board of directors that does not participate fully in company decisions, credit risk for a lender will depend heavily on the character of the individual.

A combination of the roles of president/chairman and CEO is normally frowned upon by institutional investors, but their primary concern is with large incorporated companies. For smaller companies, autocratic management by the president/chairman/CEO/major shareholder will often be crucial to the success of the company. This, after all, is how many family-run businesses have operated and flourished over time.

Strategic Positioning

When a customer asks for loans or credit extending over a number of years, the lender must give some thought to whether the customer will still be there at the end of that time. This calls for some assessment of the customer's longer-term strategic position in its markets.

Much has been published about corporate strategy, and this book will not go into this topic in much detail. Briefly, however, the medium-term strategic position of a company can be judged according to a fairly small number of criteria.

- Direction for the business
- Cash flows and profitability
- Markets and products
- Technology and change
- Competitive advantage

Direction for the Business

If a company is asking for medium-term credit from a bank, there has to be a good and convincing strategic reason for wanting the money. If funding is to have an acceptable strategic purpose, the business should have a clear sense of direction. It should know what it is trying to achieve, and how it is likely to succeed in its markets and against its competition. Financing growth is an obvious reason, perhaps, for wanting a loan, but if a company asks for a $5 million loan for a five-year term to finance an acquisition, it would be reasonable to suppose that the company could repay the loan with interest within the five-year term. Even if the money is needed to buy a new office building, there is a strategic purpose; for example to accommodate a growing administrative system to support business expansion, or to provide better service to operational divisions.

Borrowing might be a part of a conscious corporate strategy for long-term funding. When a large multinational raises funds, it should seek a suitable balance between equity funding and debt in its capital structure. It is reasonable for a finance director of a large company to ask for bank funding in order to achieve a desired mix of equity and debt.

Cash Flows and Profitability

Some companies use up cash more than others, and cash-absorbing businesses will be perceived as a more risky bet for eventual returns. A company needs at least as much cash coming in as cash going out if it is to survive in the longer term.

A business might be highly cash-generative, calling for a relatively small cash outlay on any venture before revenues are earned and profits are made. A cash-rich company will not need to borrow often, although it may have some seasonal needs. It should need just normal levels of trade credit.

With larger businesses, substantial amounts of capital spending will typically be required before projects start to pay back. Growing businesses can soak up funds as money is spent on capital expenditures and tied up in working capital. Some businesses, notably construction and property, could not survive without huge amounts of borrowing to support the cost of work-in-construction and the purchase of land or buildings.

The likely speed of payback, and the prospective profitability in relation to funds borrowed, are likely to be key issues by which a bank judges the strategic prospects for a customer's future cash flows.

In the short term, companies can report profits and still have severely negative cash flows. Cash flows are therefore more important than profits for short-term survival. In the longer term, profits are vital. If a company is unlikely to earn adequate profits, it shouldn't stay in the business. A strategic assessment of profitability calls for an assessment of a company's ability to pay loan interest out of its estimated trading profits and the potential effect on these profits (and on the company's ability to pay) from increasing competition and falling margins. The analyst ought to look not just at total sales and profits, but at:

- The size of the profit margin. A high margin business should be a lower credit risk than a small margin business (provided that its sales volume is high enough).
- Likely trends in profit margin. Big margins can be eroded by competition or adverse economic circumstances.
- Fixed costs in the cost structure. The profits of companies with a high proportion of fixed costs in their cost structure are more vulnerable to a downturn in business than the profits of companies with low fixed overheads. High fixed-cost companies should be able to cut back their costs quickly in a recession to protect profit margins.

Markets and Products

The analyst will want to be confident that a borrower's business has reasonable long-term prospects for success, because it is the profits from this business that will be expected to repay the borrowing.

A company might be viewed as a risky proposition for lending if it cannot answer yes, with reasonable confidence, to the following questions:

- Does it have good markets for its products or services?
- Does it have competitive products or services to sell, in terms of price or quality?

A strategic assessment of a company's markets and products should take into consideration:

- the size and strength of the existing markets in which the company operates, and segmentation within the market
- whether there is scope for market expansion or the likelihood of a downturn
- the customer's product range, and the extent to which it is dependent on a small number of products, or markets and customers
- the life cycle of products in the market, and the timescale within which replacement products must be developed.

It is easier to judge existing markets and products than future products or new target markets. A prospective borrower without a well-established business seeking to develop a new product in a new market will be a very high risk customer. Banks will charge a premium interest rate to small business customers, reflecting their relative exposure to these untried businesses. This practice is particularly common in times of high inflation, where the rate of default on bank loans increases.

It is difficult for an outsider to make an accurate judgement about the scope for market expansion. All too often, it is difficult for the management of the company to make this judgment themselves. A lender can only try to be aware of the potential risks. An interesting example in recent years has been the development of Psion, the UK manufacturer of hand-held computers with an international reputation. The potential for market expansion in this field would at first sight appear to be huge; however in reality, the market is vulnerable. This is as a result of both the rapid pace of change in technology, and due to market fragmentation, where a lack of standardization in computer software and hardware exists. In addition the recent entry of Microsoft into the market as a competitor has threatened Psion's position as market leader. Clearly all these issues make for a difficult lending decision for a banker.

Prospects for market expansion or decline will also often depend on the outlook for the economy. At the start of an economic downturn most companies will face some fall in business volume and profits, and the ability to survive the downturn or recession could depend on the underlying strength of the market.

Geographical Spread of Markets

Any supplier to a local market needs to provide cheaper or better quality goods or services than a competitor who serves a wider geographical area. As markets become more international, a supplier to just the domestic market is more local than international competitors, such as producers from other European Union countries. Without lower costs or better quality in their geographical market area, local companies are likely to lose out eventually to better-resourced and larger rivals.

Product Range

Although it is now more fashionable (considered good business sense) to concentrate on core industries and products, rather than to diversify into different product/market areas, companies ought to have some variety in their range of products or services. The Ford Motor Company, for example, makes motor vehicles but produces several different models. It achieves variety within a single industry.

When a company has a limited product range, such as the water or electricity utilities, it relies on a continuing market demand for its product. A producer of a small range of military equipment or a manufacturer or large engines, for example, could rely on strong demand for spare parts for repairs and maintenance of goods purchased in the past, to secure a long-term market for its products. A small producer of optical equipment, for example, still supplies replacement parts for equipment purchased over 50 years ago, and expects this market demand to continue.

Product Life Cycle

When products have a short life cycle, companies that manufacture or sell them will be under continual pressure to develop new items. The consumer electronics industry is an example. These companies could appear to the credit analyst to be fairly high medium-term risks, because it is difficult for any company, no matter how successful it has been in the past, to produce a continuous stream of new product ideas.

The Supply Chain

It could be important to understand the position of the company's products or services in the supply chain for its industry and markets. The supply chain describes the sequence of processes for turning raw materials into products for the end-consumer or end-user.

A company that specializes in one industry and operates in the middle of a supply chain is likely to be in a strategically weak position, particularly when there is strong competition in the market from rival suppliers. This has been a weakness of companies in the semiconductor industry, for example.

A company involved in the supply chain for a range of different industries is in a stronger strategic position because it is not over dependent on the strength of markets in any particular industry. Non-specialist transport services and office equipment and materials suppliers are two such examples.

Technology and Change

Technological change and innovation within an industry create both strategic opportunities and risk. Lenders should expect companies to invest in efforts to develop new ideas or to adapt to change. A strategic weakness in a company might be either failing to adapt to changes early enough or adapting to changes too soon, and making costly errors in the learning process. Judging the right time for investment in change is a management or entrepreneurial skill, which the credit analyst could find hard to judge.

Competitive Advantage

Assessment of medium-term business risk calls for some evaluation of the company's competitive advantage. A poor competitive position will indicate high business risk, whereas strong competitive advantage implies low risk.

Competitive advantage is anything that gives one organization an edge over its rivals in the products it sells or the services it offers. One form of competitive advantage for consumer products could be a large network of distributors or outlets, when competitors have smaller distribution networks or fewer sales outlets. Much of the competitive advantage which an organization might hope to achieve, however, is provided by the nature, quality and price of its products. One company's products could have a definite edge over its rivals because it is better quality, or cheaper in price. Where rival products are much alike (such as petrol and many processed foods) competitive advantage can be sought by creating a superior *brand image* and making the product seem different and more desirable than that of a rival producer.

The competitive environment within which many companies operate is characterized by the need to achieve an advantage over rivals. However, having gained a particular advantage, a company will usually find it being eroded as competitors seek to share in the obvious benefits, unless the advantage can be protected. This means that a continuous search for markets for new products must be an essential part of a firm's strategy to maintain sales and profits in the face of competition.

Michael Porter, author of *Competitive Strategy* and *Competitive Advantage*, has argued that companies should adopt a competitive strategy to achieve some form of competitive advantage, to survive in the longer term. Competitive strategy means "taking offensive or defensive actions to create a defendable position in an industry to cope successfully with comparative forces and thereby yield a superior return on investment for the firm". (Porter: *Competitive Strategy*.)

Porter identified three broad competitive strategies that a company might adopt:

- Overall cost leadership
- Differentiation
- Focus, or segmentation

Cost Leadership

A cost leadership strategy is to achieve the position of lowest-cost producer or service provider in the industry. By producing at the lowest cost, a manufacturer can compete on price with every other producer in the industry, and earn the highest unit profits.

Overall cost leadership usually depends on achieving large production economies of scale to minimize unit costs.

Product Differentiation

Whereas a cost leadership strategy seeks to win customers by providing a good basic product or service at the lowest price, a differentiation strategy seeks to raise the quality of the product, and sell it at a higher price. The customer must be willing to pay more for the superior quality.

There is a limit to what a customer will pay, and there will be a trade-off by the customer between quality and price. Differentiation strategy is therefore aimed at achieving an optimal balance for the customer between quality and price. (Quality is a term used to refer to any desirable product attributes, including customer service.) Suppliers try to provide greater quality relative to price than rivals are offering.

A better quality product can be developed in one of three broad ways:

Breakthrough products are radically different new products, offering a significant advantage over competition or a drastically lower price. Ideally, they may offer both. Breakthrough products such as major new drugs and electronics technology normally derive from an extensive research and development effort.

However, they can be high-risk developments. Eurotunnel is an example of a breakthrough product that has failed to gain the anticipated commercial success.

Improved products are not radically different to their competition but are obviously superior in terms of better performance at a competitive price. They are usually developed by incorporating recent advances in technology into an established product.

Competitive products can be developed which show no obvious advantage over others, but derive their appeal from a particular compromise of cost and performance. The car industry provides excellent examples of competitive products. Cars are not all sold at rock-bottom prices, nor do they all provide superb comfort and performance. Nearly all new makes of cars are a compromise to particular segments of the car-buying market.

There are several implications for an active differentiation strategy. The company must seek to provide superior quality and superior service, relative to price, in the eyes of consumers. It must therefore continually seek to innovate or advertise in order to stay ahead of rivals. If rivals introduce innovations of their own, the company should try to emulate them quickly. Consequently, a firm that pursues an active differentiation strategy will probably have a large research and development budget, or a large advertising budget, which could result in requests for medium-term loans or extended trade credit.

Segmentation and Focus

The third type of competitive strategy identified by Porter is a focus strategy, whereby a firm concentrates its attention on one or more particular segments or niches of the market, and does not try to serve the entire market with a single product. A focus strategy is based on fragmenting (i.e. segmenting) the market and concentrating on particular market segments. This strategy is often best suited to a firm that is trying to enter a market for the first time.

With a cost-focus strategy, a company specializes in a limited number of products, or concentrates on a small geographical area in order to keep costs to a minimum within that market segment. It then competes on price in its selected market segment. This type of strategy can be found in the printing, clothing and car repair industries.

A quality-focus strategy involves selecting a segment of the market and competing on the basis of quality (through product differentiation) for that segment. Luxury goods are the prime example of such a strategy. The risk in a focus strategy is that the market segment might not be big enough to provide the company with a profitable basis for its operations.

Although there is some business risk with any of the three broad competitive strategies, Porter argues that a firm must pursue one of them. A stuck-in-the-middle strategy is almost certain to make only low profits.

Competitive Forces

Within any industry, it should be possible to identify the nature and strength of competition. Strong competition could be a sign of a healthy and profitable industry, but a company must be able to respond to the actions and threats of competitors by offering lower prices, or better (perceived) value for money (quality) within the market as a whole or within a sizable market segment.

Several factors influence the strength of competitive forces.

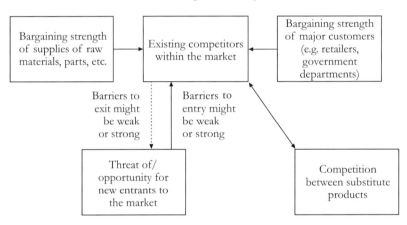

Each of these elements of competitive forces could be strong enough to weaken a company's strategic position in its markets.

Existing Competitors

There might be a large number of competitors in the market, making it difficult for any company to secure a significant competitive advantage over its rivals. The output capacity of all the producers could exceed existing market demand, creating pressures for lower prices and margins, until some companies withdraw (permanently or temporarily) from the market. In the UK, for example, the recession in the late 1980s resulted in over-capacity in the building and building supplies industries. As a consequence prices fell in the 1990s and gradually capacity was reduced as firms collapsed or shut down production facilities, such as brick-making factories.

When markets stop growing, existing producers are likely to search for ways of increasing market share. Higher spending on marketing or price cuts will contribute to lower profit margins.

In a declining market, weaker competitors are likely to go out of business. The financial problems could be particularly severe where barriers to exit from the market are high; for example, when a producer has a large investment in equipment that has no alternative use, or has to make large redundancy payments to its workforce.

Threat of New Entrants

Growing markets will attract new competitors. A significant factor for competitive forces is the ease with which new competitors can enter the market, and if their efforts don't succeed, the ease with which they would be able to pull out of the market, without incurring significant financial losses.

When barriers to entry are low, as they are in a number of service industries and in some new product markets, any company within the market is in a weak strategic position. Each company will be forced to accept ruling market prices and low profit margins. There will also be a continual search for methods of differentiating products, since new entrants to the market are themselves likely to be highly innovative. Lenders could therefore be wary of providing large medium-term loans to high margin service industries, such as advertising and design consultancies, where barriers to entry could be low.

Supplier Power

In any industry where key materials or services are provided by a small number of suppliers, producers within the industry are in a strategically weak position. They might be obliged to accept high prices for those materials or services and low profit margins for their own end-product.

Situations can occasionally arise where the sole source of supply is unreliable, perhaps where the supplier is in a politically unstable country, or where the supplier is a potential takeover target for a competitor.

Buyer Power

Similarly, where an industry is dominated by a small number of powerful buyers but there is intense competition amongst producers, there is a likelihood that prices will be kept low and profit margins will be squeezed, with the buyers exerting their bargaining strength. Some large retailers have a reputation for exerting their buyer power over suppliers, to obtain low prices and long credit periods. Suppliers to powerful buyers could therefore need more credit themselves because they are being squeezed by their major customer.

Substitutes

Competitive forces will be strong whenever customers are able to switch at a low cost from one supplier to another, or from one product to a similar substitute. Switching costs involve the expenditure of both money and effort and customers will only switch if the effect seems worthwhile. The supplier is in a stronger position to hold on to its existing customers if changing products would require staff retraining.

Assessing Strategic Power: SWOT Analysis

The assessment of a company's strategic competitive position within its markets is a qualitative exercise. For the purpose of medium-term lending the key decisions are

- Should we lend?
- If so, how much should we lend?
- For what term should we agree to lend?
- What rate of interest should be demand?
- What covenants should be placed on the lending?

These decisions will depend on whether the lender judges that the company has reasonable prospects for success in its markets in the future.

One technique for assessing strategic/competitive position is SWOT analysis. This is a structured assessment of the company's:

S   Strengths

W   Weaknesses

O   Opportunities

T   Threats

Strengths and weaknesses are internal to the company, and relate to the quality of its products, the abilities of its management, the experience or skills among its staff, operational flexibility and cost structures.

Opportunities and threats are external to the company, and relate to markets, competition and environmental influences such as government regulation and economic changes.

SWOT analysis is a simple technique, which can be used at a fairly superficial level by an external lender for credit analysis, due to a lack of in-depth information about the company.

A SWOT analysis can be summarized in a cruciform chart. A cruciform SWOT chart makes it easier to summarize and reach a judgment.

Strengths	*Weaknesses*
Opportunities	*Threats*

The findings of the strategic assessment are simply listed in the appropriate box or corner of the chart.

Example

A credit analyst's assessment of the strategic position of Alpha, a company producing software products, is as follows:

Strengths	*Weaknesses*
● High quality products ● Sales to specialist niches or segments of the market ● High profit margins ● Skilled development staff	● Poor organization for selling and distribution ● Poor liquidity ● Debtors granted long credit
Opportunities	*Threats*
● New markets opening up in the Pacific Basin and Central Europe	● Risk of increased competition from abroad. Piracy of products ● Uncertain growth prospects in existing market segments.

In this example, the analysis suggests that the company is successful in its existing market segments, earning high profit margins with high quality products. However, weak sales and distribution, some financial weaknesses and the threat of increased competition might raise some doubts about the company's ability to continue to prosper in the future, unless it exploits new markets that may be opening up.

Summary

The credit analyst should make an assessment of a customer's business, its strengths and weaknesses, and the dynamics of its industry and markets. This assessment will be based on the experience and judgment of the analyst, but should also use as much objective and factual information as is available.

Understanding the customer's business is particularly important for analysts in banks, but can also be significant for some credit decisions. Credit decisions will not usually be made on business risk analysis alone, but an understanding of the business risk reinforces an analyst's assessment of a company's financial situation and its ability to repay any credit that it owes.

Analyzing Financial Statements

The purpose of credit analysis is to reach a judgment about a customer's ability to pay. The analyst must therefore make an assessment of the company's financial position, and in particular its solvency and liquidity. Financial reports and statements about the company are a key source of information.

What Statements are Available?

Some financial statements report historical results; others are future projections. They include:

- the company's annual report and accounts
- interim statements for public corporations in the US and the UK. In the US these must be submitted quarterly and in the UK, half-yearly although in the case of larger companies it is quarterly
- the company's internal management accounting statements (for example, detailed statements of monthly or quarterly profits)
- budgets or similar financial forecasts, such as a cash budget or profits budget
- a financial forecast within a business plan.

The main advantages of an annual report and accounts are that they are audited and are readily obtainable. However, they are at least several months out-of-date.

Company accounts must be filed with the appropriate authorities in each country. In the case of the US it is to the Securities and Exchange Commission (SEC), the public markets regulator, and in the UK to the Registrar of Companies. This normally happens several months after the company's year-end.

Under EU law, only large companies are required to file a full set of accounts. Smaller companies can file modified accounts with less information, thereby reducing their potential value to the credit analyst.

The EU directive on interim reports states each listed company must prepare a report on its activities and profit and loss (income and expenses) for the first six months of each financial year. The report must be sent to either the shareholders or inserted in at least one national newspaper, not later than four months after the period end.

Stock exchanges often require interim reports to include an explanatory statement including any significant information enabling investors to make an informed assessment of the trends of the group's activities and its profit and loss. The interim statement of smaller businesses may be lacking in detail and therefore of little value to the analyst.

The most useful financial statements for analysis are the management accounts and budgets or forecasts, because these should be reasonably up to date. They give a better insight into the state of the company, what it has recently achieved and what it expects to achieve.

Whereas annual accounts and interim statements are usually readily obtainable, it is not so easy to get hold of management accounts or forecast statements for analysis, although banks are in the best position to do this. A bank can insist that as a condition of lending, the company must provide financial information before it makes a lending decision so that some credit analysis can be carried out. The bank could also call for financial information at regular intervals, either during the course of a loan agreement (to ensure that the borrower is adhering to specified loan covenants) or as a condition for continuing to provide an overdraft facility.

Information in Financial Statements

The credit analyst should be looking for information in a company's financial statements that could indicate its ability to generate enough cash to repay its debts on time. Broadly speaking, there are four aspects of a company's finances to assess:

- revenues, costs and profits
- cash flows
- assets, and their potential value
- current debts and other liabilities, such as trade creditors.

Income and profit margins are a guide to the company's viability, although profit-making companies can be illiquid and unable to generate sufficient cash. Cash flows are a critically important indicator of liquidity and credit risk, particularly in the short term. The company's assets could be significant. In the event of default by the company on a bank loan, or in the event of its failure to repay a debt, the bank or trade creditor could hope to obtain repayment from the liquidation of the company's assets. The company's liabilities are important because they show what it already owes to others.

Cash flow information is probably the most valuable type of financial information for the credit analyst. A company's bank could have the benefit of detailed cash flow records, or could be provided with a cash budget by the loan applicant. For many analysts, however, only limited cash flow information is available. In the US, companies must publish a cash flow statement within their annual accounts. However, even this does not give the credit analyst enough information, and other sources of data, such as the company's statement of income, must be used as well.

Contents of Financial Statements: Consolidated Accounts

The annual financial statements of a group of companies have several elements:

- CEO's or president's/chairman's report
- directors' report
- auditors' report
- consolidated balance sheet for the group
- parent company balance sheet
- consolidated statement of income
- consolidated cash flow statement
- notes to the accounts, providing supplementary details.

The accounts of public companies almost invariably consist of consolidated financial statements for the entire group of companies, of which the reporting company is the parent or holding company. (There is also a balance sheet for the parent company itself, but not an income statement.)

For credit analysis, it is important to recognize that a group of companies is not a legal entity. When credit is granted, the debt obligation belongs to the individual company within the group that obtains the credit. In the event of default, the lender or creditor has redress against that company, not against the group as a whole nor the parent company.

The only exceptions to this are when the parent company itself is granted the credit, (in which case the lender or creditor will take action against the parent in the event of default) or when the parent company and/or other companies within the group have provided guarantees of payment in the event of default by the borrowing subsidiary.

Example 1

Alpha, a subsidiary of Epsilon, is granted credit of up to $100,000 by Tango, and then goes into liquidation owing Tango $75,000.

Analysis

Unless Epsilon has given a guarantee to Tango for the payment of Alpha's debts, Tango can only pursue the payment of the $75,000 (or as much of the money as it can get) to an unsecured creditor in the liquidation of Alpha. Epsilon could (and quite possibly would) continue to trade after the liquidation of Alpha, unencumbered by Alpha's debts.

The point to remember is that consolidated group accounts are of limited use for credit analysis, *unless*

- the applicant for credit is the dominant trading company in the group, or
- the parent company guarantees the debts of its subsidiary, or
- the company that is asking for credit is the parent company itself (although even here, the consolidated accounts might be a poor guide for reliable credit analysis).

Example 2

Beta is granted credit of $250,000 by Sierra. Beta then goes into receivership, even though it is understood that an overseas subsidiary of Beta has a substantial amount of cash on deposit with its local bank. The cash cannot be transferred by the subsidiary to Beta because of exchange control restrictions in the subsidiary's country.

Analysis

As creditor of Beta, Sierra's only hope of eventual payment is from Beta itself, and Sierra has no right of action against the cash-rich subsidiary.

The Scope for Manipulation

There is a legal requirement in the US and across the European Union (EU 4th Directive) for a company's accounts to give a true and fair view. However, there is some scope for managerial judgment in the preparation of accounts, so that balance sheet amounts and reported income can to some extent be manipulated up or down. It is perhaps not too cynical to suggest that in the case of companies listed on the stock exchange, which are expected by shareholders to achieve a certain growth each year in earnings per share, there can sometimes be an inclination towards "short-termism" in the preparation of annual accounts.

Readers of accounts tend to assume that the figures before them are accurate. Unlike cash, profit is a man-made concept – it is an accounting invention open to subjective judgments and easy to manipulate. The degree of manipulation is controlled to an extent by the company law of each country and accounting standards.

The importance of accounting standards varies in different countries worldwide. The following accounting standards generally have a good reputation: USA, UK, Australia, Canada. Compliance with the relevant standards is required for all companies listed on a stock exchange in each country.

The International Accounting Standards Committee (IASC) has grown in reputation since its inception in the 1970s. In 1997, the IASC began publishing a series of *Interpretations of International Accounting Standards* developed by the Standing Interpretations Committee (SIC) and approved by the IASC board.

The general trend of the above accounting standard setters is to continuously tighten up the rules, allowing less manipulation of the reported financial statements. There is also a general trend towards agreement between standard setters, so that over time there are fewer differences between the different standards. This debate is often led by the IASC.

In countries with poorly developed company law and standards, there is a trend towards adoption of international standards. A problem, which is being discussed, is how to ensure that the requirements of internal accounting standards are complied with properly.

It could be argued however that despite the best efforts of the standard setters, there will always be some bending of the rules and creative accounting is unlikely to disappear entirely.

It is not the intent of this book to discuss in detail the finer points of accounts preparation. However, the credit analyst must understand, in broad terms at least, how company accounts can give misleading values, and recognize the scope for variation and manipulation that can exist. These are summarized in the following diagram.

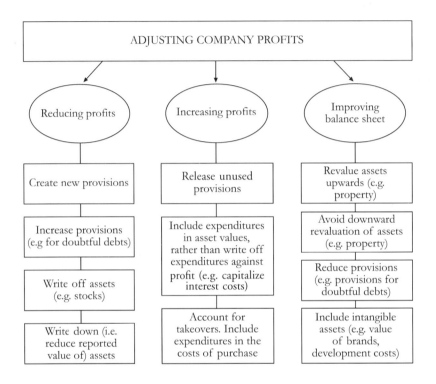

Improving Reported Asset Values

Although companies are often concerned above all else to report good profits (and earnings per share) they will also try to present an attractive balance sheet. This is particularly important for companies that want to borrow. A bank could insist on the loan agreement including a bank covenant that calls for the borrower to maintain a strong balance sheet (for example a minimum ratio of current assets to current liabilities or a minimum ratio of debts to fixed assets).

The company might therefore aim to value assets as high as possible and to report liabilities as low as possible. (It could be possible, depending on accounting regulations in force at the time, to avoid disclosure in the accounts of certain liabilities. Liabilities that are not shown in the company's balance sheet are referred to as off-balance sheet finance.)

A common method of improving asset values, more easily achieved when property prices are rising, is to revalue (upwards) freehold land and buildings, or long leaseholds.

Occasionally, a company might try to show strength in its balance sheet by creating a value for its brands. Brand accounting has its roots in takeovers, particularly within the food manufacturing, processing and drinks industries. The valuation of brands is often seen as a defense against a cheap takeover. In contrast, predator companies seeking a takeover would argue that brand valuation is simply a way for companies to make their balance sheet look better.

Examples include Diageo (formerly The Grand Metropolitan Group) and Cadbury Schweppes. These extracts are taken from the groups' 1996 annual report and accounts:

Grand Metropolitan

Fixed assets – intangible assets	Brands £m
Cost	
At 30th September 1995	3,840
Exchange adjustments	44
At 30th September 1996	3,884

The brands are stated at fair value on acquisition, denominated in the currencies of their principal markets. An annual review is carried out by the directors to consider whether any brand has suffered permanent diminution in value. Although the current aggregate value significantly exceeds the book value, no increase is made to the original value. The principal brands included above are Smirnoff, Pillsbury, Green Giant, Burger King, Häagen-Dazs, Old El Paso and Progresso.

Cadbury Schweppes

Intangible assets	1996 £m	1995 £m
Cost at beginning of year	1,689	522
Exchange rate adjustments	(142)	35
Addition	–	1,132
	1,547	1,689

Intangibles represent significant own-brands acquired since 1985 valued at historical cost. No amortization is charged as the annual results reflect significant expenditure in support of these brands and the values are reviewed annually with a view to writing them down if a permanent diminution arises.

A credit analyst should therefore consider the significance of asset valuations. Balance sheet values are not intended to indicate the prospective sale value of a company's assets. However, the balance sheet might give the best available impression of the company's asset strength. Valuations can therefore influence an analyst's assessment.

Reducing Reported Profits

A company might wish to limit its profits for the year below the amount that it could report. One reason for doing this would be, in a good performing year, to save up some profits until the next year. For example, if a company could report profits of $2.5 million in Year 1, but would be content to report profits of just $2 million, it could defer reporting $0.5 million of profits until Year 2. This would help to enhance Year 2 results.

Current year profits can be reduced in some cases by creating a provision. The purpose of making a provision is to be prudent. If there are future costs which (in the opinion of the company's directors) could be incurred as a consequence of the company's past transactions, it could be decided out of prudence, to make a charge (provision) against the current year's profits. The company therefore takes the loss before it has actually happened. A provision can be defined as an amount retained to cover any cost that is likely or certain to occur, but it is not yet certain when it will occur or how much the cost will be.

Examples are:

- A provision for doubtful debts.
- A provision for reorganization costs.

When a provision is made, it reduces profits in the current year. If it is subsequently discovered that the provision was unnecessary, or too high, it can be released at a later date. Releasing or reducing a provision adds to profits for the year.

Example
Alpha made profits of $700,000 in Year 1 and could report profits of $1 million in Year 2. The company decided during Year 2, however, that it should close one of its operating sites. Its directors decide to make a provision of $200,000 in Year 2 for planned reorganization costs.

Profits in Year 3 (after the cost of reorganization) were $700,000, and the company decided to release the provision in full to the Year 3 statement of income.

Analysis

If the company did not make the provision in Year 2, its profits would have been $700,000, $1 million and $700,000 in Years 1, 2 and 3 respectively.

By making a provision of $200,000 in Year 2 and releasing it in Year 3, the company reduces Year 2 profits and increases Year 3 profits, as follows:

	Year 1	Year 2	Year 3
	$	$	$
Income (profit) before provision	700,000	1,000,000	700,000
Provision for reorganization		-200,000	+200,000
Income (profit)	700,000	800,000	900,000

In this example, the provision enables the company to report a steady rise in profits between Years 1 and 3.

Using provisions to adjust profits between one year and the next could be used by profitable companies seeking to maintain a steady annual improvement in their results. There can be other reasons, however, for trying to manipulate the current year's profits downwards.

The ability to set up provisions on the acquisition of a subsidiary or an associated company has been restricted in the US and the UK.

On occasion, an incoming CEO might charge as many costs as possible against profits in the year of his appointment, to imply that the bad results are due to his predecessor, and that he will be able to improve results dramatically in the future. For example, by closing down a loss-making operation within the group, reducing stock values and creating a large provision for future reorganization/redundancy costs, current year profits would be reduced. However, in the next year, the excess provision can be released back to the income statement, increasing income for the year and enhancing the new CEO's reputation in the eyes of shareholders.

Increasing Reported Profits

A company might wish to increase its reported profits for the year, or at least avoid having to report a large fall in profits. There are several ways in which this can be done, (although the company's auditors must be persuaded to approve any measure that is taken). The effect of any such measure could be to:

- Release or reduce provisions that were made in earlier years (and so make use of stored-up profits).
- Avoid an increase in provisions.
- Claim revenue for the current year that could otherwise be deferred until a later year.
- Avoid having to charge certain expenditures against profits.

Releasing or Reducing Provisions

Accounts do not disclose changes in all the provisions that a company has made, and the credit analyst can only make use of whatever information is available. Provisions for doubtful debts are a particular area for some manipulation of figures.

Example 1

Beta GmBH was owed DM1 million by its customers at the end of Year 1, but made a provision for doubtful debts of 4% of this amount. At the end of Year 2, Beta again had debtors of DM1 million, but now proposes to reduce the provision for doubtful debts to 1%.

Analysis

At the end of Year 1, Beta's debtors would be reported in its balance sheet as DM960,000, which is the DM1 million owed minus the provision for doubtful debts of DM40,000 (4% of DM1 million).

At the end of Year 2, if Beta reduces the provision to DM10,000 (1% of DM1 million), there will be two effects on the accounts. First, the reported debtors will be DM990,000 (DM1 million minus DM10,000). Second, Beta's profits for Year 2 will be increased by the reduction in its provision for doubtful debts.

	DM
End of Year 1 provision	40,000
End of Year 2 provision	10,000
Increase in Year 2 profits from reduction in provision	30,000

Example 2

Gamma AG had debts of DM10 million at the end of Year 1, and made a provision for doubtful debts of 3%. Trading conditions in Year 2 were very poor, and Gamma experienced a severe problem with customer bad debts. At the end of Year 2, its debtors were again DM10 million, and it was suggested that the company's provision for doubtful debts should be increased to 5%. Gamma's management, concerned about low profits in Year 2, decided not to increase the provision.

Analysis

By deciding not to increase the provision for doubtful debts from 3% to 5%, Gamma's management avoided a reduction in Year 2 profits by DM200,000 (2% of DM10 million).

Avoiding Expenditures Against Profits

There are several methods of avoiding the need to charge some expenditures against current year profits. These usually involve adding the expenditures to the value of stock in hand or to the value of fixed assets. The expenditures become an addition to asset values rather than an immediate charge against profits. Examples include:

- Capitalizing interest costs
- Capitalizing development expenditures

Example 1

Delta Inc purchased a building for $2 million, using a 10% loan. It took six months to make the building ready for occupation.

Analysis

In the six months between purchasing the building and occupying it, interest costs on the loan to finance the purchase were $100,000 ($2 million x 10% x 6/12). Delta could decide to capitalize these costs, and value the building at $2.1 million ($2 million + $100,000 interest costs).This would avoid the need to charge the interest against profits.

Example 2

Epsilon SA spent Fr250,000 in Year 1 on developing a new product, which it plans to launch on the market in Year 2.

Analysis

Epsilon could charge the Fr250,000 against Year 1 profits, and many companies would do this. Alternatively, Epsilon could choose to report the spending as an asset in its balance sheet at the end of Year 1. It would appear as an intangible fixed asset: "Development Costs Fr250,000". None of the expenditure would then have to be charged against Year 1 profits.

It should be noted that at the time of writing, accounting standards vary with respect to policy on capitalizing interest costs. In the US, interest costs must be capitalized where in the UK, a company may capitalize interest should it wish to do so.

In respect of development costs, in the US all costs must be written off to income and expense except certain computer development costs. Under UK standards if the criteria are met they may be capitalized, whereas under IAS they must be capitalized.

Anticipating Future Income

In some cases, companies anticipate future revenue from long-term contracts as income in the current year. This can be a difficult area for judgment. For example, if a company has undertaken a two-year contract which is half-completed by the end of Year 1, the company could claim one half of the revenue and anticipated profits in Year 1, instead of waiting until the contract is finished in Year 2. A potential hazard with claiming income on incomplete long-term contracts, however, is the possibility that serious difficulties might subsequently arise with the contract, wiping out the anticipated income.

Accounting for Acquisitions

Acquisitions (takeovers) also provide opportunities for manipulating income. The accounting policies in some parts of the world that provide potential scope for manipulation include the revaluation of the assets of the newly-acquired subsidiary, making large provisions for reorganization costs and writing off goodwill through reserves. These issues are discussed below followed by the current criteria of the major accounting standards.

When one company is taken over by another, the purchasing company (the parent company) can adjust the assets of the acquired company to a fair value. Often, this means reducing their reported value.

Goodwill on acquisition is the difference between the purchase cost of the acquired subsidiary and the fair value of the assets acquired. For example, if Alpha acquires Beta for a purchase cost of $7 million, and the fair value of Beta's assets is $2 million, there will be goodwill on acquisition of $5 million.

The purchase cost, or cost of acquisition, can include not only the agreed purchase price, but also:

- Professional fees for the acquisition, and
- A provision for future costs of reorganization and restructuring after the acquisition, such as staff redundancies and relocation expenses.

For example, if Alpha buys Beta for $4.5 million, incurs professional fees of $0.5 million and provides for future reorganization costs of $2 million, the purchase cost can be reported by Alpha as $7 million ($4.5 million + $0.5 million + $2 million) rather than as the actual purchase price of $4.5 million.

Companies that include these extra charges in the cost of an acquisition will increase the amount of goodwill.

Goodwill arising from acquisitions must be recognized as an asset and then amortized over a useful life not exceeding 20 years, unless a longer life can be demonstrated. The straight-line method of amortization should be used in most cases, since it would be difficult to prove this was not the case.

The accounting standards for goodwill have developed over time. In the US, goodwill has been treated as an intangible asset for many years, with a maximum useful life of 40 years. The IASC allowed either a write off to reserves or treatment as an intangible asset until 1993, when treatment as an intangible asset became the only acceptable option. In the UK, both alternatives were allowed until 1997 after which again, only treatment as an intangible asset is allowed.

At the time of writing, a brief summary of the main provisions of each standards body is given below.

The following brief details of accounting standards apply:

Goodwill	IAS (International Accounting Standards)	FASB (US) (Financial Accounting Standards)	UK
Amortization of goodwill	Up to 20 years	Up to 40 years	Take into account on disposal
Goodwill previously written off to reserves	Ignore on disposal	Not applicable	Take into account on disposal
Reorganization provisions on acquisition	Allowed	Not allowed	Not allowed

Summary

Without going too deeply into accounting techniques, this chapter has tried to emphasize that company reports and accounts should not be taken at full face value. Figures can be manipulated, and income (profits) and asset values depend partially on management's judgment and opinion. A company's accounts remain an important source of information for the credit analyzer, but extracting relevant information often calls for a closer look at the detail. The initial, superficial picture of income and financial strength could be misleading.

To analyze a company's report and accounts (and similarly, to analyze a business plan or financial forecast) a three-stage approach might be useful.

The analyst should start with an initial cursory overview, reading through the accounts fairly quickly to look for items or features that seem to stand out. Next, he or she should check the company's approach (if it is evident) to asset valuations and methods of measuring profit, and take note of what accounting policies could have been used to manipulate profits. Finally, the accounts can be analyzed by means of key financial ratios.

Taking an Overview of Accounts

An initial impression of a company and its financial position can be obtained by reading quickly through its reports and accounts. Some items might stand out as being useful pointers to what sort of company it is and how well or badly it had performed.

Profit

There is a lot of common sense in the typical layman's approach to reading company accounts. This is to start by looking at the profit for the year, and then at what salaries the directors earned.

The profit for the year is a good starting point for analysis. Did the company make a profit, or did it make losses? Was the profit for the year just ended higher or lower than the profit in the previous year? This information is found easily enough in the profit and loss account. An analyst can perhaps get an immediate sense of whether the profit seems particularly high or low for the size of the company. A profit of $100 million might seem abnormally huge for many companies, but abysmally low for giant corporates such as General Electric or Microsoft.

Changes from the Previous Year

All companies experience some growth or decline from one year to the next. It is useful to look at the same of these changes, and in particular at the:

- Percentage change (rise or fall) in sales turnover
- Percentage change in profits
- Percentage change in fixed assets
- Percentage change in working capital (net current assets)
- Percentage change in long-term debts
- Percentage change in share capital and reserves

These increases or declines can be adjusted to allow for the rate of inflation over the period to show the *real* sales growth in the year. For example, if a company has increased its sales turnover by 8% and profits by 6%, when the annual rate of inflation has been 5%, the increases in real terms have been 3% for sales and 1% for profits.

If there has been a major acquisition or disposal during the year, there should be a large rise or fall in sales, profits and assets. Simple year-on-year comparisons can give a rough impression of what the impact of the acquisition or disposal might have been. For example, if a company has acquired a large subsidiary early in the year, and group sales and profits have risen by 25% over the previous year, it could be reasonable to presume, (prior to in-depth analysis) that much of this increase has been the direct result of the acquisition.

Directors' Salaries

The size of the salaries of directors in large companies can attract much adverse publicity, and is a source of great interest to the general reader of company accounts. For credit analysis, directors' salaries can be interesting in relation to the size of the company's profits or sales turnover.

Example
Alpha Inc. achieved profits of $500,000 on sales turnover of $10 million. Directors' salaries for the year totaled $1 million.

Analysis
A concern with Alpha Inc. could be the high level of directors' salaries relative to profits and turnover. These salaries are 200% of profits and 10% of turnover. The credit analyst should query whether, in view of the company's need for credit/borrowing facilities, the directors are taking excessive amounts of money from the company for their personal benefit.

Report of Chairman or Chief Executive Officer

The report of the chairman and/or CEO should also make interesting reading. It will normally be bullish and optimistic, but will give much information about what the company does, how the board of directors thinks the company has performed and how the company hopes to develop in the future.

Any notes of caution, or disappointment (or a stated need for extra funding) should be a warning sign. They are quite easy to spot. Any of the following comments (taken from reports by international companies) could be made by a chairman or CEO when trading conditions are tough.

- "The severe financial difficulties faced by many of our customers resulted in . . ."
- "Whilst there are some indications of better trading conditions ahead, much will depend on . . ."
- "The cost of our expansion program resulted in . . ."
- "The company is taking a number of measures to reduce costs . . ."
- "This year promises to be a challenging one . . ."
- "Your company is well placed to benefit from an economic recovery in the long term."
- "It is clear that with these developments, the group requires a new management structure."

While potential problems are not usually specified in detail, the chairman or CEO will make a guarded reference to them, to avoid any possible accusations later of neglecting to mention them or being unaware of them.

The report will almost certainly comment on any major acquisition or merger that occurred during the course of the financial year (or since the end of the financial year). Large acquisitions or mergers are significant because there is a strong possibility that the characteristics of the company (or group) will have changed. The company could be moving into a new sphere of operations. Profit margins, stock holding, the nature of fixed assets, etc. could all have altered. This could make it very difficult to compare the company's situation in the post- and pre-acquisition periods. An acquisition could have been financed largely by debt capital, thereby increasing the financial risk of the company and so altering its credit risk profile.

Extraordinary Items

A company's income statement (profit and loss account) could show an extraordinary profit or loss. Extraordinary items are distinct from the ordinary activities of the enterprise and are distinguished by the infrequency of their occurrence. The cash flows associated with extraordinary items should be disclosed separately as arising from operating, investing or financing activities in the statement of cash flows, as appropriate.

Unlike the US, in the UK a distinction is made between an extraordinary and exceptional item. Exceptional items affect the reported income (profit) from operations whereas extraordinary items do not. In the past, UK companies have often preferred to report large losses as extraordinary items. However, the regulations have been tightened up, and large gains or losses are now very unlikely to be reported as extraordinary rather than exceptional items.

Other Items to Study

It may be useful to look at several further items briefly before getting into detailed analysis of a company's accounts.

A comparison of the company's (or group's) *cash position* as at the end of the current year, and as the end of the previous year, could indicate whether there has been a noticeable improvement or deterioration of a company's performance.

The *auditors' report* is usually uninformative, and simply presents their opinion that the accounts give a true and fair view of the company's state of affairs, and that the accounts have been prepared in accordance with the relevant company legislation. Occasionally, the auditors will give a qualified report, and indicate some doubts about the validity of the accounts. On these (fairly rare) occasions, there will be a clear warning to the credit analyst that the company's situation should be studied very closely.

From time to time, out-of-the-ordinary features may appear in the company's balance sheet. These could have a bearing on the analyst's assessment. An example would be a large amount of intangible fixed assets. This could consist of brand values, development costs or the costs of patents and trademarks. The problem for the analyst is to assess whether these intangible assets are a reliable indicator of the company's value, and of its ability to generate future revenues and profits from those assets.

Another occasional item could be a property or a large investment classed as a current (short-term) asset. When a company has immediate plans to sell a major fixed asset, such as a property or a large investment, the asset could be shown in the balance sheet as a current (short-term) item and not as a fixed asset. The implication should be that the company is planning a cash sale, which ought to improve its liquidity. More information about the proposed sale should be contained in a note to the accounts.

Any note to the accounts detailing or referring to large contingencies should also be studied. Contingent liabilities are future costs that could be incurred, but the likelihood that they will arise is not yet sufficiently strong to warrant a provision in the current year's income statement. Examples are third party guarantees that have been given, or the potential damages payable in an unsettled court action. Contingencies are future payments that could be made by the company, and large contingencies would create a credit risk, because the company might not have sufficient liquidity to make these payments if called upon to do so.

Summary

Having read through the report and accounts fairly quickly, the analyst should have a general impression of the company, how well it appears to have performed, whether its position seems to have improved since the previous year and how much cash it had at the balance sheet date. Some items could have been identified for closer analysis.

The next step should be to study the accounts in more detail — a useful starting point in accounting policies.

5

Accounting Policies

The rules for preparing accounts are governed by company law. Within the US and the EU, for example, company law dictates the format in which companies must present their income statement (profit and loss account) and their balance sheet. There is also a legal requirement to apply certain fundamental concepts or principles to company accounting.

- *Going concern concept.* Accounts are prepared, and a company's assets are valued, on the presumption that it is a going concern and a viable business. Assets are <u>not</u> valued at a break-up or disposal price.
- *Matching (or accruals) concept.* This concept means that you record income in the period in which the income is earned or the benefit associated with the expense is enjoyed, rather than in the period in which the case is received or paid.
- *Conservatism (or prudence) concept.* This is the concept of conservatism in accounting. Losses should be provided for in full as soon as they are foreseen. Profits should not be claimed until it is reasonably certain that they will be earned.
- *Consistency concept.* The methods of accounting (accounting policies) that a company uses should be applied consistently from one year to the next. Accounting policies must not be changed from year to year to suit the purposes of the company and its management. If a company changes an accounting policy, the prior year's figures must be adjusted in accordance with the new policy.
- *Realization concept.* This means that earnings are not recognized until a definitive event, involving an arm-length transaction in most instances, has occurred.

Accounting Standards

In many countries company law is not specific about the detailed rules for preparing accounts, and accounting concepts are broad guidelines which leave substantial room for variation in detail and methods.

But many countries also issue accounting standards. In the US, a range of Accounting Standards is in operation, as Financial Accounting Standards Board (FASB), Generally Accepted Accounting Principles (GAAP) or International Accounting Standards (IAS). The latter apply only to public companies. Companies are expected to comply with these, and prepare their accounts in accordance with them.

Although accounting standards tighten up the rules for accounts preparation, and are more detailed than company law, they still leave companies room for the exercise of judgment in their selection of accounting policies and methods. It can be argued that accounting standards still allow companies considerable scope for manipulation of their results.

What are Accounting Policies?

An accounting policy is a method selected for the preparation of accounts, whenever there is some choice between alternative methods. Companies are required to state their accounting policies in a note to their accounts. It is important for the credit analyst to check what these are, because they can provide essential background information for the analysis of the detailed financial figures in the accounts, which may materially alter the analyst's perspective of the company itself.

Some accounting policies are more prudent or conservative than others. It is widely recognized that "company managements which report figures on a prudent basis often manage the business prudently too". Additionally, if a company's accounting appears to be conservative in matters which are clearly reported in the accounts, it is quite probable that the company will be equally conservative in the detailed areas which are less visible.

Examples of such accounting policies include:

- accounting convention and asset values
- policies for intangible fixed assets (such as accounting for research and development costs)

- stock valuations
- accounting for goodwill
- capitalization of interest
- accounting for depreciation
- accounting for foreign currencies

Accounting Convention

It is usual in the US for accounts to be prepared according to the historical cost convention, but with alternative accounting rules applied to permit the occasional revaluation of land and buildings. A policy could therefore be stated as follows: "The accounts are prepared under the historical cost convention, modified to include the revaluation of certain land and buildings, and in accordance with applicable accounting standards."

The widespread use of this convention has some implications for credit analysis.

Financial analysis of companies is carried out using the figures provided in the company's accounts. These figures include values that have been assigned to the company's assets, such as its land and buildings, plant and machinery, vehicles, investments, stocks and debtors. Normally, there is little that can be done except to take these figures at their face value, and accept them as a reasonably fair and realistic reflection of the value of the company's assets. At the same time, the analyst must also be aware that these values are not intended to show the market value or saleable value of the assets, and should not be misled by any appearances to the contrary.

The biggest problems with asset valuations relate to fixed assets. Under the historical cost accounting convention, tangible fixed assets are recorded in the accounts at their original cost. Over time and because of inflation, original cost ceases to have much meaning for fixed assets with a fairly long operational life. For example, an item of machinery that cost $100,000 in 1985 might have cost up to $150,000 if bought in 1997.

Fixed assets (with the exception of land) should be depreciated over their useful lives to an estimated residual value. Even freehold buildings should be depreciated. In the company's balance sheet, a fixed asset is shown at cost minus its accumulated depreciation (i.e. at net book value). A substantial number of companies, however, don't depreciate their buildings at all, using the argument that annual spending on repairs and maintenance is sufficient to uphold the value of the property so that depreciation charges are inappropriate. An example might be a prime retail site.

Companies can opt to use alternative accounting rules which permit a valuation at a market value (as at the last date of valuation, whenever this might have been in the past) or at a current cost (i.e. a revalued cost for an asset without an obvious market price). The option to revalue assets is commonly taken with land and buildings. Typically EU countries, other than the UK, do not take advantage of this option.

Tangible fixed asset valuations are therefore a mixture of net book value amounts, some based on historical cost and some on a revalued amount (that needn't be a recent valuation), with rates of depreciation often differing from one company to another, and in some cases with no depreciation being applied at all to property.

Intangible Fixed Assets

Intangible fixed assets create a different sort of problem with valuation. Company practice varies considerably: some companies include purchased goodwill as an asset, others report some development expenditures as an asset, and others show a value for the purchase cost of patents or copyrights. A company could create an estimated value for its brands and include this within fixed assets. A credit analyst must decide how to assess the company's intangible assets. A prudent approach might be to assume that intangibles have no value, but this approach might not be appropriate in all cases.

Accounting for Stocks (Inventory)

A company's stated accounting policy on the valuation of stock in hand is often uninformative, stating simply that stocks are valued at the lower of their original cost or their net realizable value.

Accounts give no information about the extent to which the value of stocks has been written down when their realizable value has fallen below cost. Some companies are likely to adopt a prudent approach, and write off the value of stocks which they think are unlikely to be sold or used. Other companies could continue to value stocks at cost, in spite of worries that their value might now be less. For example, a publishing company with an unsold stock of books costing $20,000 might opt to write down their value to, say, $1,000 in the expectation that very few of them can now be sold. Another similar publishing company might have opted to continue to value them at $20,000 in the expectation that they will still be sold. (The decision over the likely net realizable value should be carefully weighed up by the auditors.)

Some useful information could be obtained, however, about how stocks are valued. In particular, the valuation of work-in-progress on incomplete long-term contracts could suggest whether the company's stock valuations are conservative and lower than they could be. A tendency to minimize stock values, which is prudent and conservative, is more likely with a financially strong and robust company than with a company seeking to improve the look of its balance sheet.

Accounting for Goodwill

See Chapter 3

Capitalization of Interest

See Chapter 3

Accounting for Debtors (Receivables)

Debtors are shown in a company's published accounts at the amounts owed minus a provision for doubtful debts. Thus, one company with trade debtors of $1,000,000 might make a provision of 4% for doubtful debts, and show a value for debtors of $960,000 in the balance sheets. Another company that makes just a 1% provision would show the same gross amount of debtors at $990,000. The difference in the percentage provision for doubtful debts could be realistic, with one company suffering a higher proportion of bad debts than another. Equally, the level of doubtful debt provisions can reflect differences in prudence or caution in the approach to asset valuations.

A company will not state in its accounting policy the amount of its provision for doubtful debts. An analyst should try if possible to obtain this information (e.g. a bank might be able to get an answer from the customer directly).

Accounting for Depreciation

Depreciation can be defined as a measure of the wearing out, consumption or other loss of value of a fixed asset, whether arising from use, the passing of time or obsolescence through technological or market changes.

Depreciation is charged on the *depreciable amount*, defined by IAS4 as the asset's "historical cost or other amount substituted for historical cost (i.e. revalued amount) in the financial statements, less the estimated residual value".

The depreciable amount is charged to accounting periods, to charge a fair proportion to each period over the expected useful life of the asset.

Deciding how much depreciation to charge each year against profit is dependent on

- the cost of the asset
- its expected usual life
- its estimated residual value (i.e. disposal value) at the end of its useful life, and
- the preferred method of allocating depreciation between each accounting period. For example, an equal amount of depreciation every year (straight line depreciation method), or larger amounts in the earlier years and smaller amounts in the later years of the asset's life.

Although the cost of a fixed asset will be known, its expected useful life, its estimated residual value and the method of allocating deprecation between each accounting period are all matters for management's judgment and discretion. Management choice influences both fixed asset values in the balance sheet, and annual depreciation charges in the profit and loss account. Some companies pursue more conservative accounting policies than others, particularly with regard to estimated asset lives.

Example
Alpha Ltd has purchased a fleet of motor vehicles costing $400,000.

Two depreciation policies are under consideration. Policy A is to assume a three-year life for vehicles, and a residual value of 25% of their cost. Policy B is to assume a six-year life, and a residual value of 10% of their cost. With both policies A and B, depreciation would be charged in equal amounts each year (i.e. the straight-line method would be used).

Analysis
The choice of policy will affect reported asset values and annual depreciation costs. The policies can be compared as follows:

	Policy A $	Policy B $
Cost	400,000	400,000
Residual value	100,000	40,000
Depreciable amount	300,000	360,000
Estimated life	3 years	6 years
Depreciation costs per year	100,000	60,000

At the end of Year 1, for example, the vehicles would have a balance sheet value of $300,000 with Policy A, and $100,000 of depreciation would have been charged against profits. With Policy B, the vehicles would be valued at $340,000 and only $60,000 would have been charged against profits.

A credit analyst might take the view that vehicles ought to have a six-year life, and that Policy B is more realistic, indicating a more cost-efficient use of vehicles. On the other hand, the analyst could consider that for most company vehicles, a six-year useful life is unrealistic and too long, and that Policy B could simply be a means of minimizing depreciation charges and maximizing asset values in the balance sheet.

Accounting for Foreign Currencies

Companies must state their accounting policies for reporting foreign currency transactions or the results of their foreign subsidiaries. Accounting for foreign currencies is explained in some detail in the *Currency Risk Management* series.

For credit analysis, it can be important to recognize that when a company states its accounting policy for foreign subsidiaries or foreign currencies, it will:

- buy goods from abroad in foreign currency, or
- sell goods abroad in foreign currency, or
- have cash in foreign currencies, or
- have borrowings in a foreign currency, or
- own one or more foreign subsidiaries.

This should raise questions about the volume of the company's importing or exporting transactions, and the extent of its foreign interests. When a company is involved extensively in foreign trade or overseas operations, its profits and cash flows could be vulnerable to a movement in exchange rates.

For example, a US company that has large UK sterling earnings is vulnerable to a fall in the value of sterling against the dollar. However, it would benefit from a fall in the value of the dollar, because the dollar value of its sterling earnings would improve.

Summary

The quality of credit analysis depends on the amount of reliable financial information available. Banks are often able to insist on budgets and cash flow forecasts as a pre-condition of lending, and should be able to carry out a better analysis because they have access to the company's plans.

Without detailed budgets, cash flow forecasts or management accounts, however, the analyst has only limited financial information to work on and will rely to a large extent on the company's published report and accounts. The information in this document will probably be out-of-date and could be unreliable, depending on accounting policies used.

When the analyst has to rely on the annual report and accounts, it is important to check the company's accounting policies, to gain some insight into how the company values its assets and measures its profits. A constant question for the analyst should be: "Are these valuations reliable?"

A detailed analysis of a company's financial performance and strength will normally make use of financial ratio measurements. The techniques of financial ratio analysis are broadly the same, regardless of the quality of the financial information. Although the techniques and ratios are well-established, the analyst's judgment is crucial. What the ratios seem to be indicating depends on how the financial figures have been put together, how reliable they are and on whether they could have been manipulated to improve, superficially at least, the company's apparent performance.

An approach to ratio analysis is described in the following chapters. It is important to recognize, however, that the preliminary overview of the accounts and an appreciation of the accounting policies that the company has used should influence the analyst's interpretation of the ratios.

6

Introduction to Financial Ratios

A ratio is a measured comparison of the size or amount of one item in relation to the size or amount of another.

Ratios and percentages are widely used to analyze company accounts because they can give meaning and significance to numbers which are not so readily apparent from the detailed numbers themselves. They help to simplify an analysis and at the same time can focus on key aspects of performance.

For example, if a company has increased annual sales turnover from $42.35 million in Year 1 to $48.19 million in Year 2, it is simpler and probably more helpful to state that sales turnover has increased by 13.8% from the previous year.

If a company has profits of $1 million in the year just ended, the size of these profits cannot be assessed unless we relate this profit to the size of the company and its business, or to the amount of profit that it earned in the previous year. Similarly, if a company has current assets of $3 million, this in itself tells us nothing, until we relate this amount of current assets to the size of the company's turnover, or the value of its fixed assets or current liabilities.

The reason why ratio analysis can be so useful is that it is based on comparisons. It is only by means of comparison that performance can be properly judged.

Purpose of Ratios

The purpose of calculating a financial ratio is to obtain information about a company's financial position by comparing the ratio with:

- Trends in the same ratio for the company over a period of time: does the ratio indicate that the position is improving, stable or getting worse?

- "Standards" or "normal" ratios that are generally considered desirable.
- Ratios for similar companies in the same industry, so that the performance of one company can be judged against that of a rival, or a company in a similar sphere of operations.

Each ratio must have a particular purpose and focus on a particular issue. If it isn't clear why a ratio is being calculated, there is no point in calculating it at all.

The Variety of Financial Ratios

In practice, there are many different financial ratios that can be calculated and analyzed. Banks and companies will each have their own set of ratios that they prefer to use. The same basic ratio can often be calculated in a number of different ways, and the method chosen by analysts in any bank or company will again depend on individual preference.

This means that although credit analysts will use a number of ratios to carry out a financial analysis of a company, perhaps selecting and measuring 20 to 25 ratios, no two banks or companies will select the same group of ratios and measure them in exactly the same way. There is no official package of ratios that enjoys widespread use.

Areas for Ratio Analysis

Although a wide variety of ratios can be used, it is possible to group ratios into a few distinct categories relating to a particular aspect of the company's financial position.

In this book, ratios will be grouped into four categories:

- Profitability ratios
- Financial risk ratios
- Liquidity ratios
- Working capital and cash cycle ratios.

Suitable ratios in each of these categories can be calculated from the data in a company's financial statements. A fifth category, stock market ratios (or market strength ratios), uses share price data. Stock market ratios and their relevance to credit analysis are discussed in another title in this series, *Measuring Credit Risk*.

Can the Company Pay What it Owes and On Time?

Areas for Analysis	What could the analysis show?	Why is this important?
Profitability	How profitable is the company? How does it make profits?	A company must make profits in the long term to survive. Profit margins should be adequate.
Capital structure and financial risk	Does the company capital structure, or does it rely too heavily on debt?	A company should not be over-dependent on debt, and must be able to meet interest payment obligations out of profits. Excessive debts could force the company into liquidation if profits decline temporarily.
Liquidity	Does the company have adequate operational liquidity? Does it have adequate working capital to sustain liquidity?	A company should normally be able to generate enough cash from operations to meet its short-term operational obligations. Liquidity is crucial to survival. (However, liquidity could vary if sales volumes fluctuate seasonally.)
Uses of cash	How does the company generate and spend cash?	A company must have sufficient operational flows to pay taxation and dividends, to repay maturing loans and to contribute towards discretionary spending (e.g. capital expenditures). Inadequate cash flows result either in over-reliance on borrowing or in poor liquidity.

Computerized Systems for Financial Ratio Analysis

When a bank carries out credit analysis regularly on a number of different companies, using data from the company's accounts, it makes sense to computerize the computations. A spreadsheet package is ideal for this application. The spreadsheet can provide pre-programmed formulae for calculating the ratios. All the credit analyst has to do for the company under investigation is to key in the appropriate figures from the accounts into the appropriate cell in the spreadsheet matrix. Ratios will then be calculated automatically on the input data and printed out. Spreadsheets can also be used for simulation exercises, to ask "what if" questions about the company's financial situation and conduct a sensitivity analysis.

Although a computer program takes most of the effort out of ratio analysis, you must still be able to understand why the ratios have been calculated, what each ratio indicates, how it has been measured and how reliable or unreliable it might be.

7

Analyzing Profitability

In the long term – and perhaps in the short term too – companies must be profitable if they are to survive. Giving credit to a loss-making company will be a bigger risk than giving credit to a very profitable concern. There are in-between cases too, difficult to judge properly, where a company is making profits which are fairly small (and perhaps marginal) in view of the size of its operations and turnover.

Profitable companies can sometimes to into liquidation because their debts are too high. Nevertheless, profitability remains a key guide to the probable solvency and liquidity of a company, especially in the longer term.

The credit analyst should be particularly interested in the vulnerability of the company to a downturn in sales, and its potential consequences for profits.

Profitability Ratios

Profitability should be judged in relation to the size of the company and the volume of its business. There are three main ratios with which profits have traditionally been assessed:

- Return on assets, or return on capital employed
- Profit/sales ratio (profit margin)
- Asset turnover.

Return on Capital Employed (ROCE)

Return on capital employed (ROCE) compares the amount of profit in relation to the size of the company.

$$\text{ROCE} = \frac{\text{Profit}}{\text{Capital employed}} \times 100\%$$

Unfortunately, there are various ways of defining both profits and assets employed.

Profit may be considered to be:

- Profit before interest and tax (PBIT)
- Profit after interest, but before tax, on ordinary activities only
- Profit after tax, on ordinary activities
- Profit (before or after tax) including extraordinary items of profit or loss as well as profits on ordinary activities.

Capital employed should be:

- Stockholders funds, i.e. share capital and reserves plus long-term debt
- Stockholders funds plus total debt, i.e. long- and short-term debt and finance leases
- Stockholders funds plus total debt plus provision.

The analyst should also take a view on whether the assets of the business should include any intangible fixed assets in the balance sheet, such as brand values or development costs. The analyst should also consider the impact of any revalued assets and of goodwill written off against reserves. It is important to be consistent from year to year otherwise ratios lose their value for comparisons over time, or comparisons with other companies in the industry.

A common method of measuring ROCE is:

$$\frac{\text{Profit before interest and tax (PBIT)}}{\text{Stockholders funds plus long-term debt}} \times 100\%$$

Example

Alpha Inc. earned profits before interest and tax of $750,000 in Year 2, up from $720,000 in Year 1. The assets and liabilities of Alpha were as follows:

	Year 1	Year 2
	$	$
Fixed assets	3,700,000	5,000,000
Current assets	2,500,000	3,000,000
Total assets	6,200,000	8,000,000
Current liabilities	1,400,000	1,750,000
Total assets minus current liabilities	4,800,000	6,250,000
Long-term liabilities (debt capital)	1,250,000	1,250,000
	3,550,000	5,000,000
Share capital and reserves	3,550,000	5,000,000

Analysis

The return on capital employed in each year was as follows:

	Year 1		Year 2	
$\dfrac{\text{PBIT}}{\text{Capital employed}}$	$\dfrac{720,000}{4,800,000}$	x 100%	$\dfrac{750,000}{6,250,000}$	x 100%
	= 15%		= 12%	

In Year 2, although total profits were higher than in Year 1, there was a fall in the amount of profits relative to the size of the business. ROCE fell from 15% to 12%, suggesting a deterioration in profit performance in spite of the growth in profits and asset values.

Profit Margin

Profit margin is probably the most readily-understood financial ratio. It measures the size of profit in relation to sales turnover, and can be measured as either gross profit margin or net profit margin.

Gross margin = $\dfrac{\text{Gross profit (sales minus cost of sales)}}{\text{Sales turnover}}$ x 100%

Net margin = $\dfrac{\text{Net profit}}{\text{Sales turnover}}$ x 100%

Gross profit is the value of sales minus the costs that are directly associated with those sales. Net profit is the gross profit minus other costs, such as administrative and distribution costs. Net profit can be taken as profit before interest and taxation (PBIT), profit after interest but before taxation (PBT) or profit after taxation (PAT).

Any exceptional or extraordinary items of profit or loss would probably be ignored, because of their unusual and non-recurring nature. Whichever method of measuring net profit is used, it should be applied consistently.

Profit margins should be compared from one year to the next, and between one company and another. The analyst might want to know why one company is achieving gross margins of just 20% when a competitor is achieving 30%. Its costs could be too high, perhaps, and the company might be losing its competitiveness. Falling margins could be a concern; for example, if a company was achieving a net profit margin of 3% in Year 1 but achieved only 1% in Year 2, the fall in profit could be alarming. Indeed, a combination of rising costs and static sales prices can generally be considered to be symptoms of an economy in recession.

Example
If a company's gross profit is $11,066, sales turnover is $60,386, profit before interest and tax is $1,695 and profit after tax is $597, the profit margins in Year 1 can be calculated as follows:

$$\text{Gross margin} = \frac{\text{Gross profit}}{\text{Sales}} \times 100\% = \frac{11,066}{60,386} \times 100\% = 18.3\%$$

$$\text{Net margin} = \frac{\text{Profit before interest \& tax}}{\text{Sales}} \times 100\% = \frac{1,695}{60,386} \times 100\% = 2.8\%$$

Alternatively, net profit could be measured as profit after tax. The net margin would then be:

$$\frac{597}{60,386} \times 100\% = 0.98\%$$

The analyst could possibly conclude that these margins are very low, but it would be sensible to look at the trend in these ratios for the company over time and also to compare them with the ratios being earned by other companies in the same industry. However, a company that is making a profit before interest and tax of only 2.8c per $1 of sales is clearly operating on wafer-thin margins, and could be vulnerable to any downturn in business.

Reasons for Worsening Profitability

An analyst will be interested in the reasons for any decline in a company's profitability from one period to the next. There are two simple methods of analysis.

Company accounts could include a segmental report showing the performance of each major division or segment of the company's operations. A segmental report (giving turnover, profits and assets for each major division) is a requirement for company accounts in the US (introduced in 1976 by SFAS 14 and revised by IAS 14 and adopted as SFAS 131 in 1998) and in the UK (introduced from 1990 by SSAP25 and internationally by IAS14). Measuring ROCE and profit margins for each business segment enables the analyst to pinpoint the company's good and bad performances.

Example 1

Beta Inc.'s profits for the year were $0.75 million, achieved on sales turnover of $50 million. In the previous year, profits had been $1.2 million on turnover of $48 million. A segmental report showed the following divisional results.

| | Year 2 | Year 1 | | |
	Profits	Sales	Profits	Sales
	$000	$000	$000	$000
Agricultural products	250	30,000	700	28,000
Waste disposal services	500	20,000	500	20,000
	750	50,000	1,200	48,000

Analysis

Beta's overall profit margin fell from 2.5% in the previous year (1,200 ÷ 48,000 x 100%) to 1.5% in the current year 1 (750 ÷ 50,000 x 100%). The segmental analysis reveals that sales and profit margins were maintained in the waste disposal services division, with a profit margin of 2.5%. However, the profit margin on agricultural products fell from 2.5% in Year 1 to just 0.8% in Year 2. Clearly, this division would appear to be the cause of the company's slump in profitability.

A second method of analyzing changes in profitability from one year to the next is to compare the ratios of various items of cost to sales turnover.

Example 2
Suppose that Gamma's results are as follows:

	Current year	% of turnover	Previous year	% of turnover
	$000		$000	
Turnover	698	100	518	100
Cost of sales	(474)	-68	(333)	-64
Gross profit	224	32	185	36
Distribution costs	(27)	-4	(11)	-2
Administrative expenses	(77)	-11	(60)	-12
Trading profit	120	17	114	22
Other income	2	–	3	–
Interest payable and similar charges	(15)	-2	(6)	-1
Profit before tax on ordinary activities	107	15	111	21
Tax on profit on ordinary activities	(38)	-5	(34)	-6
Net profit after tax on ordinary activities	69	10	77	15

Analysis
Gamma's net profit margin (taking profit after tax) has fallen to 10% from 15%. This fall can be traced to specific items, by comparing the cost of each item as a percentage of sales from one year to the next. This gives the following analysis:

Higher ratio of cost of sales to turnover, (therefore lower gross margin) (68–64)	4c per $1 sales
Higher distribution costs (4–2)	2c per $1 sales
Lower administrative expenses	(1c) per $1 sales
Higher interest charges	1c per $1 sales
Lower taxation	(1c) per $1 sales
Overall reduction in profit margin	5c per $1 sales

Gamma's net profit margin (taking profit after tax) has fallen to 10% form 15%. This fall can be traced to specific items, by comparing the cost of each item as a percentage of sales from one year to the next. This gives the following analysis.

Asset Turnover

Asset turnover is a ratio that can be used to assess whether the volume of sales achieved by the company is sufficient in view of the amount of assets that it has invested in operations.

$$\text{Asset turnover} = \frac{\text{Sales}}{\text{Assets employed}}$$

Asset turnover can therefore be expressed as $X of sales per $1 of capital employed or assets invested.

Why is Asset Turnover Significant?

Asset turnover is a useful ratio because it provides an indication of how successfully the business is generating sales turnover. A higher asset turnover implies a bigger volume of sales.

Example

Using the figures earlier example and capital employed is $11,165 for Year 1, asset turnover can be measured as follows:

$$\frac{\text{Sales}}{\text{Capital employed}} = \frac{60,386}{11,165} = 5.4 \text{ times}$$

The company generated turnover of $5.40 per $1 of assets employed.

Analysis

This ratio means very little on its own, and a comparison should be made by looking at trends in the ratio over time, or at the asset turnover of other similar companies, in order to draw any conclusion.

The Year 2 asset turnover was $60,812 \div 4,298 = 14.1$ times. The difference shows an apparent improvement in Year 2 compared with Year 1. However, the improvement is so large that it would be advisable to look for the reasons behind this change before drawing any conclusion.

In this example, one reason for the change is that the company had a large amount of intangible fixed assets in its Year 1 balance sheet, much more than in Year 2. If intangible fixed assets were ignored, and Year 1 and Year 2 performance compared on what could be a fairer basis, the asset turnover ratios would have been as follows:

Year 1	Year 2
60,386	60,812
(11,165 - 8,789)	(4,982 - 268)
= 25.4 times	= 12.9 times

This suggests a large slump in asset turnover from Year 1 to Year 2, rather than a huge improvement. Another reason for the change is that capital employed has fallen due to the large retained loss in Year 2. Clearly, the analyst must draw conclusions with extreme care.

Primary and Secondary Ratios

The three traditional profitability ratios that have been described here are familiar to all analysts. They are also inter-related, and sometimes referred to as the primary and secondary ratios.

Primary ratio   **Secondary ratios**
Return on capital   =   Profit margin x Asset turnover

$$\frac{\text{Profit}}{\text{Capital employed}} = \frac{\text{Profit}}{\text{Sales}} \quad \text{x} \quad \frac{\text{Sales}}{\text{Capital employed}}$$

A company can make a return on capital of 30% by earning profit margins of 15% on relatively low asset turnover of 2.0 times. Equally, it can achieve the same ROCE of 30% by earning a low margin of 2% on a much higher asset turnover of 15.0 times. Return depends on both profit margin and sales volume: each is important for the financial health of a business.

Summary

Profitability measurements are a guide to the strength of a company's business. ROCE can be regarded as a measure of business risk. A high return could indicate low risk for a credit provider. A low ROCE could indicate high business risk, and a high credit risk. Other profitability ratios can be measured and used for credit analysis. Some will be mentioned in a later chapter, *Predicting Corporate Failure: Z scores.*

Business risk is both long and short term. Profits and sales can decline gradually over time, so that a slowly deteriorating trend in ROCE, profit margins and asset turnover can be detected. Equally, profits and sales can slump within a fairly short time period, particularly for goods or services that customers do not have to buy (e.g. consumer durables, such as furniture and kitchen goods, or motor cars). The credit analyst should consider whether a company has sufficient profit margins and assert turnover to remain financially stable in the event of a sudden downturn in business. He or she will also look to profitability as a guide to the longer-term solvency of the company.

8

Analyzing Financial Risk

Financial risk, for the purpose of credit analysis, can be described as the risk that a company will not be able to repay its debts in full or on time because its debt burden is too large. Financial risk is high when there are doubts about whether the company will have the money to pay, from any source.

Debts can be repaid from three main sources:

- cash coming into the business, mainly from trading operations
- cash raised by the company from the sale of fixed assets, stocks or investments
- new funds raised by the company, such as a new loan, or a rights issue of shares.

For lending decisions, it should normally be assumed that the opportunity to raise new funds does not exist. Granting loans for the repayment of other loans is usually bad practice.

Ratios can be used to assess a company's liability to meet its debt obligations from either of the other two sources, income from trading operations or "selling off the family silver" and disposing of assets or investments.

One concern might be whether the company has enough assets to sell off, if the necessity arose, to repay its debts. A common measure of financial risk which relates the size of debt to the value of the business is the financial leverage ratio. A second concern is whether profits will be large enough to meet the costs of interest. A second measure of risk which relates the size of interest payments to the company's trading profits is interest cover.

Leverage

Financial risk is commonly measured by leverage (or gearing in the UK). Leverage is the ratio of "prior charge capital" relative to the size of equity capital or relative to the size of total capital. Leverage can be measured in a variety of ways: here are just two.

$$\text{Leverage (or percentage)} = \frac{\text{Prior charge capital}}{\text{Equity}} \times 100\%$$

Or

$$\frac{\text{Prior charge capital}}{\text{Total capital}} \times 100\%$$

Either balance sheet values or market values can be used, for both prior charge capital and equity. Assuming balance sheet values are used, the definition of the items in the formulae are as follows:

- Equity = Common stock in issue plus balance sheet reserves.
- Prior charge capital = The balance sheet value of all longer-term capital that has a prior claim on profits ahead of equity stockholders. It consists of bank loans, finance loans and debentures under the heading in the balance sheet of "Creditors: amounts falling due after more than one year". It is also usual to include preferred stock within prior charge capital (although practice varies in this respect).

Shorter-term bank loans (with less than one year to maturity) can also be included in prior charge capital, on the assumption that the company will need to renew/renegotiate the loans for a further term, so that they are, in effect, a part of the company's longer-term funding. Certainly, in cases where a company has a large amount of debt nearing maturity, and short-term loans and overdrafts, these debts cannot be ignored when making an assessment of leverage.

Banks might therefore prefer to use a leverage defined as:

$$\frac{\text{Debt capital (short- and long-term interest-bearing debt)}}{\text{Equity}}$$

This definition of prior charge capital is not used universally by any means. Bankers could include preferred stock with equity instead of "with prior charge capital", since creditors have a prior claim on the assets of a company in a liquidation ahead of *all* stockholders, including preferred stock.

Defining leverage as the ratio of prior charge capital to equity, a company is said to be highly leveraged when the leverage ratio rises above 100%. This is when prior charge capital exceeds equity capital as a source of funds for the business.

When is Leverage Too High?

There is no "ideal" or maximum leverage level, but higher leverage indicates higher financial risk. If a company's leverage is increasing, its perceived financial risk will also rise. At some stage, lenders will decide that enough is enough, and that no further lending to the company should be granted, unless at very high rates of interest.

An important advantage of the leverage ratio is its widespread use. Bankers, financiers, accountants and other businessmen and professionals all generally understand what leverage means. There is also likely to be a feeling "in the market" about what constitutes high leverage (or excessive leverage) in the current economic and business climate. For example, in the late 1980s, leverage of 200% might have been regarded as high but not intolerably so; however, in harsher economic climates, lenders would be wary about companies with even 100% leverage. As with other ratios, trends in the ratio over time can be a useful indicator of improving or deteriorating credit risk.

Example 1
Delta is a company with common stock and reserves of $300,000, and interest-bearing debt of $100,000. It approaches its bank with a request for a $50,000 loan.

Analysis
The leverage ratio of Delta is currently 33.3% (100,000 ÷ 300,000 x 100%). The new loan would increase leverage to 50% (150,000 ÷ 300,000 x 100%). Although leverage would increase sharply, the bank might take the view that it would still be within acceptable limits. If so, it would not reject the loan application on grounds of financial risk.

Example 2
Returning to the example in the Appendix, the change in the leverage of the company from one year to the next can be analyzed.

Definition of leverage

	At 31 December Year 2	At 31 December Year 1
Long-term debt	1,834	2,565
Equity	2,450	7,934
	= 74.9%	=32.3%
Total interest-bearing debt	5,259	8,835
Equity	2,450	7,934
	= 214.7%	= 111.4%

Workings

	$000	$000	$000	$000
Bank loans due after 1 year	1,616		2,336	
Hire purchase/finance leases	218		229	
		1,834		2,565
Overdraft	192		3,549	
Bank loans due within 1 year	3,112		2,487	
Hire purchase/finance leases	121		234	
Short-term loans		3,425		6,270
Total interest bearing debt		5,259		8,835

Analysis

In spite of a sharp reduction in the company's debts, leverage rose between Year 1 and Year 2. This is because the company's equity also fell. Significantly perhaps, leverage is much higher when short-term debts are taken into account than when they are ignored (in Year 2, leverage is 214.7% when short-term debts are included, compared with 74.9% when only long-term debts are considered). This indicates a heavy reliance on short-term funding by the company. The Year 2 leverage level is very high, and the company is a high financial risk for any creditor.

Priority for Creditors in a Liquidation

As an alternative to (or in addition to) measuring the leverage ratio, an analyst could look at the potential consequences for a would-be lender in the event of the company's liquidation.

The priority list for payment of debts in a liquidation in the US (according to the 1978 Bankruptcy Reform Act) may be summarized briefly as follows:

1. Secured creditors with a fixed charge on specific assets, insofar as the secured assets realize enough money to cover the debt;
2. Liquidation expenses must then be paid before any other creditors. This can sometimes annoy creditors, for example where liquidation expenses are large due to a business failure on a grand scale;
3. Creditors (i.e. creditors who must be paid ahead of others in the list with the exception of 1 and 2 above. These include debts due to the Internal Revenue Service (IRS), unpaid value added tax and some unpaid wages and salaries of company staff);
4. Secured creditors with a floating charge on assets of the company;
5. Unsecured creditors;
6. Preferred stockholders;
7. Common stock stockholders.

Remember, however, that a balance sheet does not show the *realizable* value of assets. Nor does it indicate which assets are secured or the amount of preferential creditors. Checking the creditors' priority list is of only limited value unless a reasonable assessment can be made of what the company's assets would fetch in a forced sale.

A bank will be reluctant to lend, however, and a supplier might be reluctant to grant extensive trade credit, when a company's gearing is high and the loan or trade credit would rank low in the list of creditors to be paid in the event of liquidation.

Interest Cover

The interest cover ratio is a measure of financial risk which is designed to show the risk in terms of profit rather than in terms of capital values.

The interest cover ratio monitors the ability of the company to meet its interest commitments. It is the possibility of a company failing to pay interest that represents the main danger of high gearing. Interest cover is therefore an important measure of credit risk.

The increase cover ratio is measured as follows:

$$\frac{\text{Profit before interest and tax (usually ignoring any exceptional items)}}{\text{Interest charges}}$$

The interest cover ratio shows whether a company is earning enough profits (before interest and tax) to pay its interest costs comfortably, or whether its interest costs are high in relation to the size of its profits. If interests costs are high in relation to profits before interest and tax (PBIT), any fall in profits could leave the company unable to meet its interest payment obligations, and in danger of being forced into liquidation.

An interest cover of two times or less would be very low and cover of three times would also be regarded as low. Cover should be above three times before the company's interest costs would be considered within acceptable limits. Most treasurers finance directors and analysts look for interest cover of five times or higher. However, as with most ratios, a low interest cover in one year might be a temporary problem that will soon disappear as profits rise or interest costs fall. A low and deteriorating interest cover ratio from one year to the next would be much more worrying.

Banks often include a covenant on interest cover within a lending agreement, requiring the borrower to maintain an interest cover of a minimum specified level.

Interest cover focuses on interest payments (including interest payments on hire purchase and finance lease obligations). It doesn't consider the payment or repayment of the principal amount of the loan or a trade debt.

Example
In the example in the Appendix, the interest cover of XYZ Inc is as follows:

	Year 1	Year 2
$\dfrac{\text{PBIT}}{\text{Interest charges}}$	-4,028	1,648
	955	736
	= -4.2 times	= 2.2 times

Profit before interest and tax is calculated here by taking the profit or loss before tax, and adding back interest payable and similar charges (Year 2: -4,983 + 955 and Year 1: 912 + 736).

Analysis
In Year 1, the interest cover was dangerously low, at 2.2 times. The risk was realized in Year 2, as profits before interest and tax were turned into losses. In Year 2 there was a loss exceeding interest payments by 4.2 times. It is also possible to spot (from note 1 to these abbreviated accounts) that the company paid a further $158,000 in interest (we do not know in which year) that has

been included in the cost of stocks. This capitalization of interest has avoided the need to include these costs within interest charges in the profit and loss account. This suggests that the interest cover position is even worse than the ratios would seem to indicate. Adding interest to the costs of assets, i.e. capitalization, thereby avoiding an immediate charge against profits, can be considered to be "creative accounting" that should not be overlooked.

Debt Ratio

For the analysis of a potential customer for credit, another useful financial risk ratio is the debt ratio. This is a measure of the percentage amount of the company's total assets (fixed and current) that are being financed by credit of one sort or another.

$$\text{Debt ratio} = \frac{\text{Total creditors (due for payment either within one year or after more than one year)}}{\text{Net fixed assets + total current assets}}$$

Trends in this ratio over time can be monitored. A higher ratio indicates a higher financial risk. A ratio in excess of 50% indicates a high level of total borrowing, but there is no "ideal" maximum debt ratio within which companies should try to operate.

Example

The company XYZ Inc in the Appendix has the following debt ratios.

	At December 31 Year 2	At December 31 Year 1
Creditors (short and long term)	(21,874 + 2,041)	(20,446 + 2,931)
Assets (fixed and current)	(3,782 + 23,020)	(13,848 + 17,763)
	= 89.2%	= 74.0%

Analysis

The debt ratio was high in Year 1 at 74%. It worsened to 89% at the end of Year 2. This indicates that creditors are financing too much of the company's business. This company is clearly a high credit risk. Any request by its purchasing department for even more trade credit or for extra bank loans ought to be met with (at the very least) a strong reluctance, and in all probability a flat refusal.

In the previous chapter, profitability ratios were described as a measure of a company's business risk. It is perhaps useful to note that a company's return on equity (profit as a percentage of stockholders' funds) can be described as a product of business risk and financial risk, as the formula below shows:

$$\underbrace{\frac{\text{Profit}}{\text{Equity}}}_{\textbf{Return on equity}} = \underbrace{\left[\frac{\text{Profit}}{\text{Sales}} \times \frac{\text{Sales}}{\text{Capital employed}}\right]}_{\textbf{Business risk}} \times \underbrace{\frac{\text{Capital employed}}{\text{Equity}}}_{\textbf{Financial risk}}$$

Financial risk is not shown here as leverage (prior charge capital ÷ capital employed). However, the ratio of capital employed to equity is a similar measure of financial risk, since prior charge capital plus equity capital equals total capital employed.

In addition to business risk and financial risk, the credit analyst should also look at a company's working capital and liquidity.

Summary

Financial leverage, interest cover and the debt ratio are all useful indicators of a company's ability to pay its debts. There is no readily-identified limit, above or below which the financial risk becomes excessive. As with most ratio analysis, the analyst's judgment is needed to reach an assessment of the risk.

Analyzing Working Capital and Liquidity

In this chapter, we shall look at two different but related aspects of a company's financial position. These are its working capital structure and its liquidity.

What is Working Capital?

Working capital is a term used frequently in business but not always properly understood. One common misconception is that working capital is money coming into a business. It is not. Money coming into a business is cash flow.

Working capital is the capital invested by a business in its working assets. The investment consists principally of stocks, work-in-progress and debtors. These are assets that will (at some time in the fairly near future) provide the business with cash from its trading operations. Stock will be sold and debtors will pay what they owe.

There is a connection between working capital and cash flow that will be described in more detail later. Briefly, however, a business must buy stocks and incur expenditures in selling its goods or services before it eventually receives payment from customers. Working capital must therefore be invested to maintain stocks and debts until the cash eventually flows in.

The amount of working capital that a business needs can be reduced by taking short-term credit. An investment in stocks, for example, is not required if suppliers give credit; the investment is needed only when stock has to be paid for.

The following diagram represents the assets and the sources of finance for a business. Assets are either long-term fixed assets or short-term current assets.

Current assets can be defined for the purpose of this chapter as stocks and debtors. Sources of finance consist of long-term funding (from share capital and reserves, and long-term loans) and short-term liabilities, which can be defined for the purpose of this chapter as short-term creditors. Working capital is the difference between short-term assets and short-term liabilities. It is the amount by which short-term assets are financed by long-term funds.

A Company's Assets and Liabilities

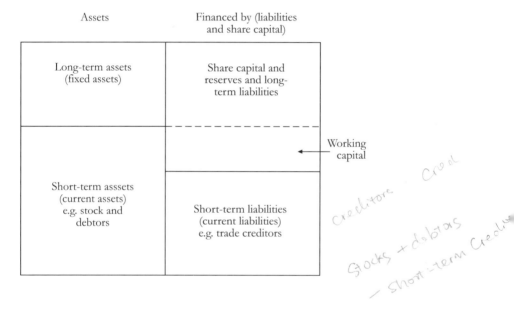

Assets

Financed by (liabilities and share capital)

Long-term assets (fixed assets)	Share capital and reserves and long-term liabilities
Short-term asssets (current assets) e.g. stock and debtors	Short-term liabilities (current liabilities) e.g. trade creditors

Working capital

Working capital is strictly an amount of funding. In practice, it is more convenient to discuss working capital in terms of the current assets and current liabilities themselves. In other words, working capital is commonly regarded as the amount of stocks and debtors of the business minus the short-term creditors.

Stocks, debtors and creditors continually change. Stocks are used or sold on credit. Debtors pay what they owe. Suppliers are paid. New stocks are purchased, and new sales are made. The value of stocks, debtors and creditors is never a fixed amount. The working capital a company needs therefore fluctuates as its stocks, debtors, cash balances, creditors and bank overdraft change in amount. This fluctuating amount of assets and liabilities must be managed. The working capital needs of a business can vary depending upon the maturity of the product portfolio.

Let us consider companies that need to make a relatively high investment in working capital. Kværner, the international engineering and construction group is a good example. Year end 31 December 1996 accounts reveal current assets of NKr27.8 billion ($3.5 billion) against current liabilities of NKr29.2 billion. When one appreciates the sector within which the group is operating, the NKr600 million working capital investment is understandable. Shipbuilding, processing industries and construction are all capital intensive industries, typically with long production lead times.

Why is Working Capital Significant?

For the credit analyst, working capital is significant for three main reasons.

- A company could have an excessive amount of working capital, in particular stocks and trade debtors. This would be an inefficient and wasteful use of capital. When a company seeks a bank loan to finance an increase in its current assets, the analyst should therefore check whether the extra assets are really necessary.
- A company could have insufficient working capital. This could be due to an over-reliance on short-term liabilities, in particular trade credit and a bank overdraft to finance its current assets. A bank or supplier should consider whether it is appropriate to continue extending credit to the company, where an injection of longer-term finance (e.g. new equity) might be more appropriate.
- There is a connection between a company's working capital and its cash flows and liquidity, matters of prime concern to the credit analyst. Cash comes in from selling stocks and from payments by debtors. Cash goes out to pay creditors. There must always be enough cash coming in to meet the payments going out.

Working Capital, the Trade Cycle and the Cash Cycle

Key elements of working capital for a trading company are stocks, trade debtors and trade creditors. These exist because there is a trade cycle and an associated cash cycle. The trade cycle starts with the purchase of resources (materials, labor, etc.) and ends with the sale of a finished product or service to the customer. Trade is a continuous cycle of buying and selling.

The cash cycle starts with the payment for purchased resources and ends with cash receipts from sales to customers. There is a continuous cycle of cash out – cash in – cash out, etc. Payment from customers allows the company to pay its suppliers, and purchase more raw materials, etc., so that the trading cycle can continue.

The trade cycle and the cash cycle do not coincide, because credit is taken from suppliers and given to customers. The trade and cash cycles of a typical manufacturing company are shown below.

Trade Cycle and Cash Cycle of Manufacturing Company

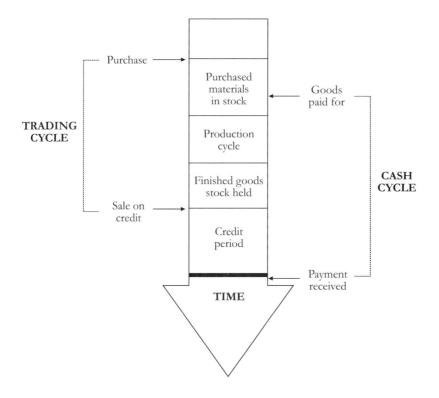

Both the trade cycle and the cash cycle can be measured by time. The cash cycle describes the average period of time that elapses between the payment for the purchase of raw materials, components or supplies by a company and the eventual receipt of cash from customers who buy the finished goods or services. In short, it is the average time between paying out cash and getting cash in from trading operations.

This is shown in the table below.

Cash Cycle and Trade Cycle Times

		days
	Raw material held in stock	A
+	Production cycle	B
+	Finished goods held in stock	C
=	Trade cycle	A + B + C
-	Time to pay creditors	-D
+	Time for debtors to pay	E
=	Cash cycle	A + B + C - D + E

The cash cycle and the size of a company's working capital investment are directly connected with each other. A longer cash cycle means a bigger investment in working capital.

Example 1
Alpha sells $10,000 of goods on credit each month, and gives customers two months to pay. Trade debtors therefore average $200,000. Alpha's management is considering whether to extend credit and give customers three months to pay.

Analysis
If customers are given three months to pay, the cash cycle will become one month longer and trade debtors will increase to $300,000. A bigger investment in working capital, by $100,000, will therefore be needed.

Example 2
Beta buys $50,000 of materials each month and takes one month (30 days) credit. It therefore owes an average $50,000 to its suppliers. If then asks its suppliers for extended credit terms, with two months to pay from the invoice date.

Analysis

If Beta's suppliers agree to the request, Beta's trade creditors will increase to $100,000. The cash cycle will now be shorter (by one month). Less working capital will be needed because the increase of $50,000 in trade creditors will help the company to finance its current assets.

A company could have an excessive investment in working capital. Its cash cycle could be too long because it allows debtors too much time to pay, or it has a very low stock turnover, or it doesn't take long enough credit from suppliers.

In contrast, a company could be trading with insufficient working capital (a situation referred to as overtrading). Its cash cycle could then be too short, especially when it takes very long credit from its suppliers but allows its own customers only a short time to pay. Overtrading is described in more detail in the next chapter.

Cash Cycle Ratios

The length of a cash cycle can be estimated by three ratios or time measurements:

- average stock turnover. This is usually measured in days
- creditor days. This is the average period of credit, in days, taken from suppliers
- debtor days. This is the average period of credit, in days, given to customers

The average stock turnover time plus debtor days minus creditor days equals the cash cycle duration

Stock in days	+ Debtor days
- Creditor days	Financing gap in days

These three ratios can only be approximated from information in a company's published accounts, and the ratios will not be exact. However, if the ratios are measured consistently over time, trends in the length of the cycle will become apparent, and significant changes identified. In some cases, there could be a generally-accepted "normal" cash cycle within an industry. Ratio analysis should be a practical and effective method of identifying when any company in an industry has an excessively long or short cycle compared to others.

The three ratios are measured as follows:

Ratio	Meaning	Measurement
Stock turnover	Average period of time for which stock is held between purchase and eventual sale of the end-product or service	$\dfrac{\text{Stocks in hand}}{\text{Cost of goods sold}} \times 365 \text{ days}$
Creditor days	Average length of credit period obtained from suppliers	$\dfrac{\text{Trade creditors}}{\text{Cost of goods sold}} \times 365 \text{ days}$
Debtor days	Average length of credit period given to customers	$\dfrac{\text{Trade debtors}}{\text{Sales}} \times 365 \text{ days}$

A figure for the cost of goods sold is used to calculate the stock turnover period and creditor days. This figure is obtainable from a company's accounts (in the profit and loss account, or in a note to the accounts). A principle in ratio calculation should be to match like with like, above and below the line. Stocks and trade creditors are valued in the balance sheet at cost, and the best available estimate of the total cost of stock purchases in the year is the cost of goods sold.

Debtors, in contrast, are valued in the balance sheet at their invoiced amount, and it is therefore more suitable to have annual sales turnover as the figure below the line to measure an approximate average for debtor days.

Example 1
Gamma Inc.'s results are as follows:

	For the year	Per month
	$	$
Sales	120,000	10,000
Cost of goods sold	60,000	5,000
Gross profit	60,000	5,000

Average stocks are $10,000, average trade creditors $5,000 and average debtors $40,000. The company is faced with growing pressure from customers for longer credit.

Analysis

Gamma's cash cycle and working capital investment can be estimated as follows:

	Cash cycle			Working capital investment
		(days)		$
Stock turnover	$\frac{10,000}{60,000}$ x 365	61	Stock	10,000
Creditor days	$\frac{5,000}{60,000}$ x 365	(30) 31	Trade creditors	(5,000) 5,000
Debtor days	$\frac{40,000}{120,000}$ x 365	122	Debtors	40,000
		153		45,000

An increase in debtor days, say from 122 days to 150 days, would result in an increase in average debtors from $40,000 to about $49,000 (150 ÷ 365 x $120,000). The company would then need extra working capital funding of $9,000. Alternatively it could try to take extra credit from suppliers, or borrow $9,000 more on overdraft.

Example 2

It would be more accurate to estimate the company's "average" stocks, creditors and debtors as the midway value between the current year (Year 2) and previous year (Year 1) balance sheet values; however end-of-Year 2 figures are used here, to simplify the numbers.

Analysis

The cash cycle ratios are as follows:

Year 2			Workings	
				days
Stock turnover	$\frac{\text{Stocks}}{\text{Costs of goods sold}}$	x 365	$\frac{7,871}{58,785}$	49
Creditor days	$\frac{\text{Trade creditors*}}{\text{Cost of goods sold}}$	x 365	$\frac{10,897}{58,785}$	(67)
Debtor days	$\frac{\text{Debtors}}{\text{Sales}}$	x 365	$\frac{12,487}{60,812}$	75
				57

Year 1			Workings	
				(days)
Stock turnover	Stocks	x 365	5,838	43
	Costs of goods sold		49,320	
Creditor days	Trade creditors	x 365	(8,697 + 86)	(65)
	Cost of goods sold		49,320	
Debtor days	Debtors	x 365	11,412	69
	Sales		60,386	
				47

The company has experienced an increase of 10 days, (from 47 to 57 days), or over 20%, in the length of its cash cycle. A credit analyst would need to take a view of whether this is a significant change and whether the cash cycle is becoming too long. Alternatively, the cash cycle could originally have been too short and is now closer to normal. Comparisons with other firms in the industry would provide useful information for making these judgments.

Liquidity

Efficient working capital management can optimize a company's cashflow cycle and its investment in working capital. A company should also have adequate liquidity, i.e. ready access in the short term to sufficient cash for its needs.

Liquid assets are cash or other current assets that in the near future either can be turned into cash (if required) or will become cash in the normal course of trading.

A company must have sufficient liquid assets in the short term to meet its current payment obligations as they fall due. Alternatively, a company could borrow, probably on overdraft, to pay what it owes, but a bank will want to ensure that a company does not rely too heavily on an overdraft facility (or other debt funding) to maintain adequate liquidity.

When deciding whether to grant credit or make a loan to a company, liquidity is a prime factor. Liquidity risk is the crucial short-term credit risk. A company must have cash now to pay immediate obligations. The promise of cash in the future to repay debts is of little interest when the payment is due now.

Liquidity and Working Capital

Liquidity can be analyzed through working capital. To do this, it will help to think of working capital as the amount of long-term capital invested in current assets, to fund the company's cash cycle or trading cycle. It is therefore the amount of current assets that is not funded by current liabilities.

A balance sheet can be represented by the basic formula:

$$D + SF = FA + WC$$

Where:

Long-term funds
D   =   long-term debt
SF   =   stockholders' funds

Assets minus current liabilities
FA   =   fixed assets
WC   =   working capital

This formula may be fairly simple, but it can be used to make several useful observations about a company's financial position. The formula shows that long-term debt plus shareholders' funds together (D + SF) must provide the finance for the investment in fixed assets and working capital. (FA + WC).

Suppose that a company needs more. With reference to the formula, there would be three possible sources of working capital funding. It could raise new funds (and increase either D or SF by the amount of the increase in WC). It could retain some profits in the business (increase SF by the amount of the increase in WC). Or it could reduce its fixed assets (FA). This could be achieved by failing to replace fixed assets as they get older or by disposing of some for cash.

More significantly, perhaps, there are three ways in which working capital can be reduced. Again, reference to the formula will suggest how this can be achieved. The company could repay some long-term loans (reducing D) and in doing so be forced to cut its investment in WC. It could incur trading losses (reducing SF). Losses force a company to reduce its fixed assets or working capital. Or it could buy more fixed assets (increasing FA) and be forced to reduce its working capital to finance the purchases. When working capital is reduced, the company must either cut down the amount of its current assets, or it must increase its current liabilities, perhaps by increasing its bank overdraft or taking more credit from suppliers. This could threaten its liquidity.

Example
A company has current assets of $120,000 and current liabilities of $70,000. Its working capital is $50,000. It wishes to buy new fixed assets for $10,000 and decides to reduce its working capital to finance the purchase.

Analysis

To reduce working capital by $10,000, the company could cut its stocks and debtors by $10,000 to $100,000. Alternatively, it could take more credit from suppliers or increase its bank overdraft, to raise current liabilities to $80,000. In reducing working capital, the company will be either cutting its cash-producing assets or increasing its short-term liabilities. Either way, it will be putting more pressure on its cash flows.

This is where the connection between working capital and liquidity comes in. Liquidity means having enough cash or near-cash assets to meet payment obligations. Current assets must generate sufficient cash to pay for purchases and pay off any bank overdraft.

Liquidity Ratios

Liquidity ratios compare the amount of the company's liquid assets with its short-term requirements to pay creditors.

Liquid assets, i.e. assets that are cash or will soon be turned into cash, can be defined in several ways, but the most commonly used are either:

- total current assets (including stocks), or
- current assets excluding stocks.

Stocks are generally less liquid than debtors and other current assets. In some cases, however, such as supermarkets selling consumer non-durables, stock is very liquid, with a short shelf life and a rapid turnover. Defining liquid assets should depend on just how liquid the stocks are in the business of the particular company.

A liquidity ratio compares a company's liquid assets with its short-term debts (current liabilities). The most commonly used liquidity ratios are the current ratio and the quick ratio (or acid test ratio).

Current Ratio
The standard test of liquidity is the *current ratio*. This is the ratio of:

$$\frac{\text{Current assets}}{\text{Current liabilities*}}$$

* Creditors: amounts falling due within one year

The idea behind this ratio is that a company should have enough current assets that give a promise of "cash to come" to meet its future commitments to pay off its current liabilities. This suggests that the current ratio should be higher than 1:1. If current assets did not exceed current liabilities, there would be the prospect that the company might be unable to pay its debts on time. In practice, a ratio comfortably in excess of 1:1 should commonly be expected, but what is "comfortable" varies between different types of businesses. In industries where it is normal to pay creditors after stocks have been used and resold, such as in supermarket retailing, a current ratio of less than 1:1 would be comfortable.

Quick Ratio or Acid Test Ratio

Companies are usually unable to convert all their current assets into cash very quickly. In particular, some manufacturing companies might hold large quantities of raw material stocks or have a long production cycle (e.g. aircraft production). Stocks of finished goods could be warehoused for a long time prior to sale. In such businesses, where stock turnover is slow (most stocks are not liquid assets) because the cash cycle is so long. For this reason, an alternative liquidity ratio, known as the quick ratio or acid test ratio, might be more useful for analysis.

The *quick ratio*, or *acid test ratio*, is:

$$\frac{\text{Current assets less stocks}}{\text{Current liabilities}}$$

This ratio should ideally be at least 1:1 for companies with a slow stock turnover. For companies with a fast stock turnover, however, a quick ratio can be comfortably less than 1:1 without suggesting that the company should be in cashflow trouble. This is because stocks are relatively liquid assets.

Are there Ideal Liquidity Ratios?

Both the current ratio and the quick ratio offer an indication of the company's liquidity position, but the absolute figures should not be interpreted too literally. It is often theorized that an acceptable current ratio is between 1.5 and 2.0, and an acceptable quick ratio is around 0.8 to 1.0, but these should only be used as a guide. Different businesses operate in different ways. One supermarket chain, for example, can operate comfortably with a current ratio of 0.44 (year-end 8 March 1997 figures), and quick turnover, particularly in view of stock perishability), and more trade creditors than stocks. This suggests that stock is resold before it is paid for – a common trait in the retail trade.

What is important is the trend of the ratios. From trends, the analyst can judge whether liquidity is improving, deteriorating, or stable. If the supermarket had traded profitably for the past 10 years with current ratios of 0.44 and quick ratios of 0.18, it should comfortably continue with those levels of liquidity. If in the following year its current ratio were to fall to 0.29 and its quick ratio to 0.03, then a further investigation into the liquidity situation would be appropriate. It is the relative position that is far more important than the absolute figures.

And don't forget the other side of the coin either. A current ratio and a quick ratio can get bigger than they need to be. A company that has large volumes of stocks and debtors might be over-investing in working capital, and tying up more funds in the business than necessary. This would suggest poor management of debtors (credit) or stocks by the company.

Example
The current ratio and quick ratio of XYZ Inc are as follows:

	Current ratio		Quick ratio	
31 December Year 1	$\frac{17,763}{20,446}$	= 0.9	$\frac{11,925}{20,446}$	= 0.6
31 December Year 2	$\frac{23,020}{21,874}$	= 1.1	$\frac{15,149}{21,874}$	= 0.7

Analysis
In this example, the company's liquidity could seem low. A comparison with other firms in the industry would be helpful. However, there was some improvement in liquidity in Year 2, compared with Year 1.

The Usefulness of Liquidity Ratios

The current ratio and quick ratio are useful in several ways. They can be used to obtain year-on-year comparisons and identify trends in the company's liquidity position. They can be used for comparisons of working capital and liquidity with other companies in the same business sector or industry.

Companies cannot safely afford to have a poor current ratio because bankers and suppliers could interpret this as an indication of credit risk.

It is important to recognize, though, that the current ratio and quick ratio are not exact guides to liquidity. Current liabilities could have maturities that range from "very soon" to "up to one year away". Bank overdraft facilities can be renewed, and thus have an even longer maturity in practice.

Even a higher current ratio, which ought to be a sign of good liquidity, could be a cause of liquidity difficulties for a rapidly expanding company. As the company's business grows, it will need much more working capital to support the growth than a company that can operate with a low current ratio.

Inverse of Current Ratio

Although the current ratio is commonly used, a credit analyst could prefer to look at the inverse of the current ratio:

$$\frac{\text{Current Liabilities (CL)}}{\text{Current Assets (CA)}}$$

This shows the proportion of current assets that are being financed by current liabilities. If the CL:CA ratio is 60%, for example, 60% of current assets would be financed by current liabilities, leaving 40% financed as working capital by long-term funds of the business.

No Credit Interval (NCI)

Other ratios can be used to monitor liquidity. An interesting alternative is the No Credit Interval or NCI. This can be defined as an estimate of the length of time that a company could finance the expenses of its business, at its current level of activity, by drawing on its own liquid resources and on the assumption that it made no further sales.

Put another way, it is based on the view that current assets, with the exception of stocks, will soon be realised into cash. Similarly, current liabilities must soon be paid. The difference, net current assets minus stock levels, should soon be available in cash to the company. The size of this surplus can then be compared against the volume of the company's regular expenditures. The formula for the NCI is as follows:

$$\frac{\text{Current assets (excluding stock) minus current liabilities}}{\text{Daily operating expenses}}$$

Daily operating expenses can be estimated from the company's accounts as:

(Sales - Profit before tax - Depreciation and amortization) ÷ 365

Depreciation and amortization are deducted because they are not cash expenditures.

Example 1
Alpha Inc. has current assets excluding stocks of $500,000 and current liabilities of $200,000. Its annual operating expenses, estimated as sales minus pre-tax

profits and depreciation, are $7,300,000.

Analysis

Daily operating expenses are $20,000 ($7,300,000 ÷ 365 days). The NCI is therefore ($500,000 - $200,000)/$20,000) = 15 days. The company has sufficient liquidity in its working capital to finance expenditures for 15 days. This could be regarded as a comfortable liquidity position.

Example 2

We can calculate the NCI for XYZ Inc.

	Year 2	Year 1
	$000	$000
Sales	60,812	60,386
Profit before tax (add back loss)	+4,983	-892
	65,795	59,494
Depreciation and amortization (note 1 to the accounts: Year 2 = 474 + 108 and Year 1 = 453 + 313)	-582	-766
Annual operating expenses	65,213	58,728
Daily operating expenses in $000 (÷365)	178.7 per day	160.9 per day
	$000	$000
Current assets	23,020	17,763
less Stocks	-7,871	-5,838
less Current Liabilities	-21,874	-20,446
	-6,725	-8,521
No Credit Interval =	-6,725	-8,521
	178.7 per day	60.9 per day
=	-38 days	-52.9 days

Analysis

In this example, the NCI is negative. This indicates very poor liquidity, although there is evidence of an improvement in liquidity between Year 1 and Year 2. A company with a low current ratio and a low quick ratio will have a negative NCI, whenever current liabilities exceed current assets excluding stocks.

Summary

A company's cash cycle and liquidity should be analyzed for evidence of short-term credit risk. High profits, low leverage and high interest cover are evidence of long-term financial strength, but adequate liquidity is essential in the short term.

In addition to what can be termed operational liquidity, i.e. liquidity arising from cash generation, it is worthwhile investigating what contingency funding could be available to the company should it be required. Bank overdraft facilities can be called in or cancelled at any time by the lenders and could represent high vulnerability for a company with liquidity problems. However, companies with committed medium-term bank facilities providing funding for up to five years are far less vulnerable to temporary liquidity problems, provided that these facilities have not yet been fully utilized.

Cash flow information can also be obtained from cash flow statements.

Cash Flow Analysis

Cash flow analysis can be used to assess the creditworthiness of a customer both from historical accounting information about cash flows, and also by preparing forecasts of a customer's future cash flows.

Cash Flow and Credit Analysis

Cash flow is important because a company must be able to generate cash to pay its debt obligations, such as interest and loan principal. There are four sources of cash generation:

- *Operational cash flows.* This is cash generated from the operational activities of the company. A credit analyst will want to see signs of operational cash flow strength in its customer's business.
- *Operational flexibility.* This is the ability to liquidate an asset or sell part of the business to raise cash to repay a debt, if the necessity arose.
- *Financial flexibility.* This is the ability to raise extra funds in the financial markets, or to refinance maturing debts. (Financial risk analysis, such as the analysis of gearing ratio and interest cover, can be used to assess a company's current financial flexibility.)
- *Guarantees from a third party.* A bank could have recourse to a third party guarantor (e.g. a parent company) in the event of default on loan repayments by a customer.

A creditor such as bank will look to one of these sources for repayment and the principal source will normally be operational cash flows. If a company can't pay what it owes from what it earns, it could have very serious financial problems. A widely-held view amongst bankers, therefore, is that there should be at least one other source for repayment, should the primary source dry up or fail.

Cash flows, unlike profit and loss accounts and balance sheets, are not easily "colored" by window dressing and creative accounting. Information about cash flows is therefore more likely to be reliable than information about profits, asset values and shareholders' reserves.

What is Cash Flow?

Cash flow can be defined in a number of different ways. A simple example might help to explain the various definitions.

Example
A company, Alpha Inc., is established on December 31 Year 1 with a share capital (all subscribed for in cash) of $5,000. In the year to December 31, Year 2 the company raised an extra $2,000 by issuing new shares. It also borrowed $4,000.

Fixed assets costing $10,000 were purchased, and the depreciation charge on these was $1,500 for the year. Stock costing $12,800 was purchased during the year. At December 31 Year 2, $2,500 of this stock was not yet paid for. Sales for the year were $20,000, of which $3,000 were unpaid debtors at the year end. Unsold stock at the year end had a cost value of $800. Wages and salary costs and other cash expenditures, all relating to the Year 2 accounting year, were $4,000. Interest charges, all paid, were $400.

Cash in hand at the end of Year 2 was $3,300.

Analysis
The income statement for the year to December 31 Year 2 was as follows:

	$	$
Sales		20,000
Cost of Sales	(12,800 – 800)	12,000
Gross Profit		8,000
Wages, etc.	4,000	
Depreciation	1,500	
Interest	400	
Other costs		5,900
Net profit before tax		2,100

The balance sheet of the company can be prepared, for both the end of Year 1 and the end of Year 2.

| | At December 31 Year 1 | | At December 31 Year 2 | |
	$	$		$
Fixed assets				
Cost				10,000
Less depreciation				1,500
Net book value				8,500
Stock		800		
Debtors		3,000		
Cash	5,000	3,300		
		7,100		
Trade creditors		2,500		
Net current assets				4,600
				13,100
Bank loan				(4,000)
	5,000			9,100
Share capital	5,000			7,000
Profit and loss account				2,100
	5,000			9,100

Analysis

Cash flow can be defined as net cash flow, traditional cash flow, or operational cash flow.

Net cash flow is the net change in the cash position between the beginning and the end of the period. In this example, there has been a change in cash held, from $5,000 at December 31 Year 1 to $3,300 at December 31 Year 2, giving a negative net cash flow of $1,700. Net cash flow is of little information value, however, unless its component elements or causes are analyzed.

Traditional cash flow is a rough-and-ready estimate of cash flow from operations. It is calculated on the assumption that cash flow can be estimated by adding back non-cash items of cost to the net profit. Non-cash items of cost are mainly depreciation. In this example, traditional cash flow would be calculated as follows:

	$
Net profit	2,100
Add depreciation	1,500
Traditional cash flow	+3,600

This is an *inflow* of cash. Traditional cash flow has the advantage of being easy to calculate and is often accurate enough for a credit analyst's requirements. A more accurate calculator of operational cash flow can be time-consuming and fairly complex.

Operational cash flow is the actual cash flow from trading operations during the period. It will normally exclude finance charges, but could include them. Here, excluding the interest payment which is a finance charge, we have:

	$
Cash flow from sales (20,000–3,000)	17,000
Cash paid for purchases (12,800 – 2,500)	-10,300
Cash paid for wages, etc.	-4,000
Operational cash flow	+2,700

A *categorized cash flow* sets out the entire cash flows of the business, not just cash flows from trading operations. The categories will be chosen to suit the requirements for analysis. In this example, they might be:

	$
Cash flow from sales	17,000
Cash paid for purchases	-10,300
Cash paid for wages, etc.	-4,000
Interest payments	-400
Fixed asset expenditure	-10,000
Bank loan	4,000
Issue of shares	2,000
Net cash flow	-1,700

A categorized cash flow gives the component elements of net cash flow.

Cash Flow: Operational, Priority, Discretionary and Financial

Although cash flows can be categorized in any way to suit the credit analyst, a method of categorization that might be preferred gives four groupings: operational, priority, discretionary and financial. According to the international newspaper, the Financial Times (December 27, 1996): "It is important to recognize that there is no correct definition of cash flow, just as there is not a single measure of profit. But just as investors distinguish between operating profit, pre-tax profit and earnings, it is important to be precise about which sort of cash flow one is talking about".

Operational cash flows have been defined above. In the example, these came to +$2,700 in total, but could be sub-categorized between receipts from customers, cash payments for purchases, wages payments, etc. Operating cash flow is often defined as earnings before interest, tax and depreciation and amortization (EBITDA), except that adjustments are made for working capital. It is called "cash flow from operating activities", in US and cash flow from operations in UK cash flow statements. While working capital changes can be significant in an individual year they tend to even out over time.

Priority cash flows are payments for non-trading cash items that must be made to keep the company afloat, and have priority over non-operational items. These priority items are all cash outflows. They include interest payments and tax payments. They could also include the repayment of principal on maturing debt. Once priority cash flows have been met, the remaining cash flow is often referred to as free cash flow.

Discretionary cash flows are cash payments or receipts that do not have to be made. Discretionary cash payments could be deferred if necessary and some discretionary income could be earned if required. They include:

- Discretionary outflows: capital expenditure, payments for acquisitions, the purchase of financial investments, payout of ordinary dividend and preference dividend
- Discretionary inflows: the sale of fixed assets, the sale of subsidiaries and the sale of financial investments

Some discretionary outflows would be regarded as more urgent than others. For example, there might be a minimum desirable amount of capital expenditure or a requirement for an ordinary dividend payment. For projecting future cash flows, some capital expenditure could have been committed already.

Some analysts also refer to *residual cash flows*. This is defined as free cash flow minus dividends. It is the amount available for repaying debt and acquisitions. Often, residual cash flow is a negative amount. It is not terribly useful for valuation purposes, (from the analyst's perspective), but in judging how much debt and dividends a company can support, it is invaluable.

Financial cash flows arise from variations in long-term capital. Financial inflows include cash from the issue of shares, or from new loans. Financial outflows include the repayment of debt principal (it not included as a priority outflow), the repurchase of some of its own shares by a company or the redemption of other long-term instruments.

Operational Cash Flows: the Cash Tank and the Cascade Effect

To a credit analyst, the main consideration is the customer's need for cash, and the ability to pay promptly what is owed. In the case of bank loans, interest and possibly principal repayments are priority cash flows for the customer. They have to be met by cash inflows from at least one of the other three sources:

- operational cash flows
- net inflows from discretionary items
- net inflows from long-term financing sources.

Operational cash flows will often be the source of cash from which all or most other cash payments can be made, in a descending order of priority. It might be helpful to think of operational cash flows as water going into and out of a water tank. The tank represents the company's operations.

- The tank must be kept full of water, so that cash inflows are sufficient to meet cash outflows
- If operational cash flow is positive, and cash inflows exceed outflows, the tank will overflow
- The surplus water (cash) falls into a tray beneath the water tank, representing priority cash flows. When these have been paid, and the priority cash outflow tray is full, the surplus will overflow again into a lower tray, representing discretionary cash outflows

It could be described as a cascade effect, with the surplus cash outflows at one level and moving down to the next level for cash outflows.

Cash Tank

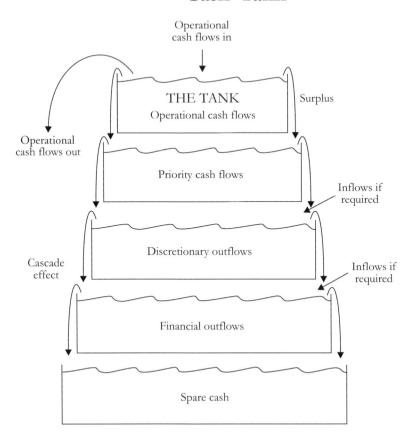

When operational cash flows are insufficient, a "top-up" of cash will be needed from discretionary or financial sources (or by using existing cash in hand).

There will be times when operational cash flows are insufficient to meet other cash needs. There could even be a deficit in cash flows from operations. These situations will occur, in particular when a company is expanding its operations rapidly, when it wishes to finance a large capital expenditure or acquisition, or when it must repay the principal on a large maturing debt.

Operational Cash Flows: Profitability and Working Capital Management

Operational cash flows were described earlier as the net cash flows from a company's trading operations. Credit analysts are particularly interested in this cash flow category because operational cash flows are normally the primary source for repayment of loan interest and repayment of principal.

When a company has high profit margins, and its sales turnover is either stable or growing slowly, there should normally be very few operational cash flow problems. The company should have enough cash coming in to meet the payments it must make.

Operational cash flow problems are much more likely to occur when the company is making only small profits, or trading at a loss. Problems can also occur when the company is growing too fast and is overtrading (i.e. is under-capitalized and "out-stripping its asset base").

It is important to recognize that a company can make losses but still have a net cash income from trading. A company can also make profits but have a cash deficit on its trading operations. Trading profits and cash flows are different. One reason for the difference is that non-cash items of cost such as depreciation will make trading profits lower than operational cash inflows. A second reason for the difference is changes in the amount of the company's stocks, debtors and creditors.

A simple illustration helps to make this point. Suppose that a company buys and resells products. Gross profit from trading and operational cash flows from trading can be compared as follows:

Profit	Operational cash flow	
Sales	Cash in	$\left\{ \begin{array}{l} \text{Sales} \\ \text{+ Opening debtors} \\ \text{- Closing debtors} \end{array} \right\}$
- Cost of sales	- Cash out	$\left\{ \begin{array}{l} \text{Cost of sales} \\ \text{+ Closing stock} \\ \text{- Opening stock} \\ \text{= Purchases} \\ \text{+ Opening creditors} \\ \text{- Closing creditors} \end{array} \right\}$
= Profit	= Operational cash flow	

Profit is sales minus the cost of sales. Operational cash flow is the difference between cash received and cash paid from trading. Cash received differs from sales because of changes in the amount of debtors. Cash paid differs from the cost of sales because of changes in the amount of stock and creditors. Operational cash flow therefore differs from profit because of changes in the amount of debtors, stocks and creditors between the start and end of a period.

Example
Assume that Beta Inc achieved sales turnover in a particular year of $200,000

and the cost of sales was $170,000. Stocks were $12,000, creditors $11,000 and debtors $15,000 at the start of the year. At the end of the year, stocks were $21,000, creditors were $14,000 and debtors $24,000.

Analysis
Profits and operational cash flows are different, as follows:

	Profit	Operational cash flow
	$	$
Sales	200,000	200,000
Opening debtors		15,000
Closing debtors		(24,000)
Cash in		191,000
Cost of sales	170,000	170,000
Closing stock		21,000
Opening stock		(12,000)
Purchases		179,000
Opening creditors		11,000
Closing creditors		(14,000)
Cash out		176,000
Profit/operational cash flow	30,000	15,000

The difference between profit and cash flow has important implications for credit analysis. If a company is profitable but short of cash, one reason could be an increase in working capital. The credit analyst should ask whether this increase was necessary.

If the company in the example were to seek credit from a bank to finance the growth in working capital, the bank might ask the management whether operational cash flows could be improved by squeezing working capital, and

- reducing debtors
- reducing stocks, or
- taking more trade credit from suppliers.

Better control over working capital could remove the need to borrow.

If a company is making losses, it could try to maintain a positive operational cash flow by taking more credit (i.e. by increasing its creditors and so reducing working capital). The credit managers of supplier companies should then consider whether to give the extra credit required, or whether to refuse because the risk would be too great.

The Overtrading Company

When a company is expanding rapidly, it could operate at a profit but still suffer from a cash flow problem because of the requirement for growing quantities of working capital to finance the expanding business.

Companies that grow quickly and are unable to finance the additional working capital from operational cash flows are said to be overtrading.

Example

A company that buys and resells products achieves the following results:

	$
Sales	140,000
Cost of sales	120,000
Trading profit	20,000

Average stock = $1/6$ of the annual cost of sales

Average trade creditors = $1/12$ of the annual cost of sales

Average debtors = $1/4$ of annual sales

Analysis

If the company maintained annual sales and costs at this level, its operational cash flows would bring in $20,000 of cash each every year.

If the company doubled its sales in the subsequent year, and working capital turnover periods (i.e. the cash cycle) remained the same, the company would have negative operational cash flows of $5,000, as follows:

	Effect on cash flow
	$
Trading profit (20,000 x 2)	40,000
Increase in stocks	- 20,000
Increase in debtors	- 35,000
Increase in trade creditors	+ 10,000
Operational cash flow	-5,000

If the company continued at this rate of expansion, its operational cash flows would remain negative. This, of course, is before we even consider the need for cash to meet priority outflows and desirable discretionary outflows, for capital expenditures and dividends.

Overtrading can therefore indicate a cash flow crisis, in which the company is living "hand to mouth", collecting cash from debtors as quickly as possible and making creditors wait for payments as long as possible. A request for more trade credit from a customer in this situation should normally be refused. Similarly, a bank that is asked for a larger overdraft facility by an overtrading company should either refuse, or charge a rate of interest that the high-risk, nature of the lending would warrant.

The cure for overtrading is to avoid rapid growth and to consolidate the business after any period of fast growth before expanding any further. This is the advice that a bank should given when confronted with a customer in this situation.

Negative Operational Cash Flows: Implications

Negative cash flows from operations would normally be an indicator of financial distress, unless the company is in a period of rapid (and profitable) growth and is having to invest heavily in additional working capital (stocks and debtors).

If a company has negative cash flows from operations for at least two of the previous three years, it will probably be safe to conclude that its financial position is deteriorating significantly.

Cash Flow Statements

Cash flow statements are required in the financial statements if companies report under US, UK and IAS standards. The formats of each are slightly different but the purpose of all these statements are the same, i.e. to show how cash has been generated and how it has been spent.

The US and IASC standard requires reconciliation to cash and cash equivalents. A cash equivalent is a financial instrument which is within three months of maturity when it is purchased. The UK standard requires reconciliation to cash only. These minor differences in format do not significantly affect the analysis of these statements.

The following example is based on the US Generally Accepted Accounting Principles (GAAP).

Example XYZ Inc
Cash flow Statement Under US Accounting Standards

	19X1 $m	19X0 $m
Cash flow from operating activities		
Net income	74	82
Adjustments to reconcile net income to net cash provided by operating activities:		
Provisions for credit and other losses	25	8
Accretion of unearned interest and deferred net fees	(45)	(28)
Undistributed earnings of equity method affiliates	(2)	(2)
Net realized gains on sales and other dispositions of assets	(4)	(4)
Net unrealized losses (gains)	1	(24)
Net deferred income tax provision	12	7
Net change in trading account assets	(316)	115
Net change in amounts with holding company and subsidiaries, net	(41)	44
Net change in accrued interest and other receivables	(5)	93
Net change in accounts payable	26	(39)
Net change in other liabilities	(55)	(12)
Total adjustments	(369)	(241)
Net cash (used in) provided by operating activities	(295)	323
Cash flows from investing activities:		
Net change in interest-earning deposits with banks	279	277
Net change in federal funds sold	(1)	274
Proceeds from sales of available for sale securities	819	636
Principal collected on held to maturity securities	78	207
Net change in loans	(577)	(552)
Net change in amounts with holding company and subsidiaries, net	153	181
Proceeds from sales of land, buildings and equipment	354	12
Purchases of land, buildings and equipment	(18)	(22)
Sale of affiliates	–	–
Net change in other assets	9	112
Net cash provided by investing activities	140	709
Cash flows from financing activities:		
Net change in customers' deposits	378	(634)
Net change in short-term borrowings	140	(62)
Net change in amounts with holding company and subsidiaries, net	(242)	(43)
Proceeds from issuance of long-term debt	389	–
Principal repayments of long-term debt	(292)	(281)
Transfer of long-term debt	(87)	–
Cash dividends paid on common and preferred stock	(114)	(26)

Net cash provided by (used in) financing activities	172	(1,046)
Effect of exchange rate changes on cash and non interest-earning deposits with banks at the beginning of the year	13	5
Net change in cash and non interest-earning deposits with banks	30	(9)
Cash and non interest-earning deposits with banks at the beginning of the year	259	268
Cash and non interest-earning deposits with banks at the end of the year	289	259

Key Points

Only cash transactions are recorded. Therefore if an acquisition of a company is undertaken for a total consideration of $10 million, which is settled by $5 million in shares and $4 million in cash, only the $5 million cash will impact on the cash flow statement.

The layout prioritizes what a company needs to do with its cash so that its financial health can be judged. A company which cannot cover its interest, dividends and tax liabilities out of its operating cash flows cannot expect to sustain that position for long without getting into serious financial difficulties. Most people, on the other hand, would be reasonably sympathetic to a company which borrowed money to invest in new fixed assets.

The overall increase/decrease in cash position needs to be compared with the position at the beginning of the year.

Interpretation of Cash Flow Statements

Cash flow problems do not usually happen overnight. They build up over time, and an analysis of historical cash flows and trends over the past few years can be very instructive.

Cash flow analysis begins with the company's ability to generate profits and goes on to assess the ability of the company's management to manage cash and finances in addition to making profits. In particular, key questions are:

- how much cash is the company generating from its operations?
- is this enough for the company's needs?
- is it possible to make estimates or projections of the company's future cash flows, in order to improve the assessment of its creditworthiness?

Cash flow statements can be studied by looking at the absolute size of the cash flows. Most significant is the amount of cash flow from operations, after paying interest, tax and (if any) dividends. This amount of net cash flow should be the source of much of the company's capital expenditure funding, as well as the means to repay the loan principal.

Ratio Analysis

Ratios can also be used for analysis. Since cash flow analysis will focus mainly on operational cash flows, it is useful to calculate the ratio of operational cash flow to other items of cash flow. This is to assess the strength of the company's operational cash flows relative to the size of its need for cash for other (non-operational) purposes.

Operational Cash Flow and Priority Cash Flows (Interest and Taxation)

The ratio of operational cash flow to priority cash outflows, sometimes referred to as the *debt service ratio*, measures the ability of the company to pay its priority outflows from operational cash flows. Operational cash flows should be comfortably in excess of priority payments.

$$\text{Debt service ratio} = \frac{\text{Operational cash flows}}{\text{Priority cash flows}}$$

The debt ratio has similarities with the interest cover ratio, since interest payments are one of the main priority cash flows. A ratio of less than 2.0 would be "uncomfortable", to say the least.

Operational Cash Flows, Priority Cash Flows and Dividends

It is often assumed that a company's directors will use operational cash flows to pay dividends to shareholders whenever the opportunity arises. A further ratio for analyzing the adequacy of operational cash flows is:

$$\frac{\text{Operational cash flows}}{\text{Priority outflows (interest + tax) + Dividends}}$$

This should be analyzed in the same way as the debt service ratio. If the company expects to pay a dividend, its operational cash flows should be well in excess of the combined cost of the priority outflows and the dividend payment. A ratio above 2.0 is desirable.

Capital Expenditure (Capex)

Capital expenditure (capex for short) is important for virtually all businesses because it involves cash outlays "now" to generate operational cash inflows in the future, and to keep the company in business for the longer term.

Capex has been referred to here as a discretionary cash outflow. To some extent, it is. Unless contracts have been signed and expenditure is committed, capex plans can be deferred or scrapped.

In all businesses, however, some capital expenditure is essential to keep the business going at its current level; fixed assets must be replaced eventually. A difficult task for the credit analyst is to judge what minimum level of capex seems necessary for the business, and how much of the "discretionary" outflows are really essential.

In some industries, the reduction or cessation of capex could take many years to work through to damaging the financial performance of a company. An automobile manufacturer is an example of a company where, ultimately, an inability to invest can be a threat to survival, given the need for investment in new car models.

At the very least, a minimum capital expenditure should be equal to the annual provision for depreciation in the profit and loss account. With price inflation, the cost of replacing fixed assets will normally exceed the original cost of the "old" assets. It is therefore not very contentious to suggest that annual capital expenditure should, as a minimum requirement, be higher than the depreciation charge in the profit and loss account.

Internal Financing Ratio

It is certainly reasonable to suppose that in the long term (but not necessarily year-by-year) a company should be able to finance most of its capital expenditures from its own operational cash flows, with only a smaller proportion financed by new borrowing, even allowing for dividend payments to shareholders.

In other words, in the long term, operational cash flows minus priority cash flows and dividend payments should be about the same amount as capital expenditure outflows. All we are saying here is that a company should be able to finance most of its capital expenditures internally.

A suitable ratio for measuring a company's performance on this issue is the internal financing ratio:

$$\frac{\text{Capital expenditure cash flows including payments for acquisitions}}{\text{Operational cash flow minus priority cash flow and dividends}}$$

This ratio can be greater than or less than 1:1 in any particular year, but in the longer term, it ought to be fairly close to 1:1 on average. If it is greater than 1:1, the company will be using new borrowing to finance some of its capital expenditure programme. Just how much capital expenditure is being financed by borrowing is obviously of great interest to the credit analyst.

Summary

Cash flow is crucial to business survival or failure. Although cash can be obtained from several sources, such as raising new capital or selling off parts of the business, the key source of cash, in the longer-term at least, must be from trading operations.

Cash flow analysis can be used to assess the adequacy of a company's cash flows, and to identify potential problems, such as overtrading or excessive capital expenditure commitments.

The strength of ratio analysis is that it makes comparisons possible:

- of ratios over time (trends)
- with other, similar companies
- occasionally, against a standard, ideal, maximum or minimum "safe" ratio.

Indequate ratios could indicate high credit risk.

Using Ratios

The previous chapters have described a range of financial ratios and suggested the purpose of each ratio, and what it could signify for the analyst. There is the problem, however, that when a range of financial ratios has been calculated, the information has to be evaluated, to enable the analyst to make a recommendation or decision about giving credit to the company. The analyst should judge whether additional credit can be given to the company with reasonable safety, or whether the company, without additional credit, might "fail".

Business failure could mean:

- "technical" insolvency, where a company is unable to meet its maturing obligations (e.g. the redemption of a loan)
- "real" insolvency, where the liabilities of the company exceed its assets (and if this is more than a temporary situation, the company will inevitably go into liquidation)
- legal insolvency or bankruptcy (i.e. going into liquidation)

Weaknesses of Ratio Analyst

The strength of ratio analysis is that it gives the credit analyst a means of assessing the financial situation of a company by condensing the information about the company into a few key ratios. Ratio analysis, however, has some drawbacks.

It cannot easily be used to predict what will happen in the future to the company under review. Some models have been developed for predicting corporate failure by means of ratio analysis, but these are not universally used, nor are they 100% reliable.

Because it draws on just a few key figures from a company's accounts, ratio analysis ignores all the other information that a set of accounts could provide – hidden away perhaps in the lengthy details of the notes to the accounts.

A further difficulty with ratio analysis is that the different ratios could provide conflicting indicators. A company could have good profits but high leverage, low interest cover but strong operational cash flows, or high profits but low liquidity. Many companies are neither in an extremely strong nor an extremely weak position, and the analyst will often be looking at companies somewhere in the middle. Reaching a conclusion about whether to give credit (and if so how much) will depend ultimately on judgment, reinforced by evidence that investigating the business and its financial position can provide.

Analysts who study companies regularly can develop a structured approach to their analysis, based perhaps on:

- a points scoring system
- an analytical questionnaire, or
- "what if" scenario building

Points Scoring

Points-scoring systems for credit analysis could be used by a bank to assist with lending decisions. Banks, understandably, are reticent about their use of these systems, and their details. The principle behind points scoring, however, is that some financial ratios are more significant than others. Points can be allocated to each of a number of key ratios, according to their perceived significance. Companies can then be given a score, up to the maximum allocated, for each of these ratios. A lending decision can then be made depending on whether the company's total score for all the ratios exceeds or falls short of a certain level.

Points-scoring systems have much in common with corporate failure prediction models (described in the next chapter). They can be rigid, but provide a discipline for credit decisions that can be important for large lending banks. Their main drawback is their doubtful reliability: the key question is whether they can improve the quality of lending decisions, and their effectiveness has not been clearly proved.

Symptoms of Failure Questionnaires

It is often small points of detail that give a clue about whether the company's directors are consciously trying to make the profits seem better or worse, and asset values higher or lower, than perhaps they probably ought to be reported.

Ratio analysis can take an analyst so far, but a closer analysis of the accounts would be desirable to give a more complete picture.

In many cases, companies that have collapsed unexpectedly have been large, reputable and seemingly well managed. The failure of the international company Polly Peck and British niche retailer Sock Shop are two examples. On an international scale, the collapse of the merchant bank Barings, seemingly a rock solid British institution, shocked the world. The UK's oldest merchant banking group was placed into administration after the Bank of England failed to put a rescue package in place. Barings had been a victim of losses caused by massive, unauthorized dealings undertaken by one of its traders in Singapore. The loss wiped out the bank's capital of £541 million, including £336 million of non-voting equity shares held by the family's Barings Foundation Charitable Trust.

An analysis of past corporate failures has revealed common symptoms such as:

- fast and aggressive expansion, especially when accompanied by a sharp rise in borrowings
- dominant personalities at the head of the company, often combining the roles of chairman and CEO. (Boardroom strife and the resignation of one or more directors are often a "leading indicator" of trouble for the company)
- relative youth of the company. Companies are more vulnerable to collapse in their earlier years
- the use of "creative accounting" techniques, especially reserve accounting (by which losses are written off directly against reserves and not reported through the consolidated statement of income).

These common signals of corporate failure can be combined together to form a rough-and-ready system for assessing a company by looking at its annual report and accounts. Symptoms of corporate failure are shown in the following questionnaire:

Symptoms of Failure Questionnaire

1. Is the same person holding the posts of chairman and CEO?
2. Is the financial gearing ratio over 100%?
3. Has gearing increased significantly since the previous year?
4. Is there a greater amount of short-term borrowing than long-term borrowing?
5. Are there signs of rapid expansion, so that turnover has grown by more than 50% per annum over the past five years?
6. Did turnover more than double either last year or the year before?
7. Has the company recently made, or it is planning to make, a move of premises?

continued over page

> 8. Have any directors resigned?
> 9. Is the report and accounts a lavish (expensive) production?
> 10. Is the company in a cyclical industry?

Using this model, it has been shown that if the answer is yes to more than five of these questions, the company should be viewed with some caution, and if the answer is yes for eight or more questions, there should be no investment in the company without making a more thorough investigation.

"What If" Scenarios

Ratios lend themselves readily to spreadsheets and microcomputer modeling. A spreadsheet file can hold the financial data about a company over a number of years (or months), making the task of tracking trends over time quite simple.

An even greater advantage of spreadsheet models is the ability to analyze possible future scenarios and asking "what if" questions about changes in the future financial position of a company, namely a sensitivity analysis. For example, with the latest financial data for a company on a spreadsheet file, an analyst can assess the effect on the company's position if it were to obtain $X of extra trade credit to finance stocks, or if its profitability were to fall so that the net profit margin fell to Y%, or the effect on interest cover if interest charges rose by Z%.

The ability to ask "what if" questions also gives the credit analyst the opportunity to gauge the consequences of a continuation of past trends. Thus ratio analysis can become a forecasting tool as well as a monitoring process on past performance.

Summary

A problem in credit analysis is how to use all the information about a company that can be collected. Judgment will normally be required, and experience should help to improve the quality of the analyst's judgment.

A view exists, however, that available information can be analyzed and condensed into a prediction of a company's future creditworthiness. The most widely publicized methods of predictive analysis are corporate failure prediction models, such as Z-score models.

Predicting Corporate Failure: Z Scores

A difficulty with financial ratio analysis is the large number of ratios that have to be monitored, and the absence of any definitive rules about how to identify danger signals in the ratios that are calculated. In many cases, ratios for a company could give conflicting indications, such as a company with good liquidity, and low gearing but low profitability. How should these be assessed?

Credit decisions can depend heavily on the experience, judgment and opinion of the analyst, rather than on objective facts.

Difficulties with interpreting a range of financial ratios have prompted the question: "Is there a single ratio or value that can be calculated which indicates the financial situation of a company, which an analyst can rely on to make a judgment?"

Corporate Failure Prediction Models

Some researchers have developed models, based on ratio analysis, which can be used to identify companies that might be "at risk" (in danger of failure or being taken over, or in serious need of restructuring or improvement).

Research has been carried out to discover whether financial ratio analysis (and trends in the variations of ratios over time), can be used to predict business failure or businesses at risk. This research can be divided into two categories:

- models which try to identify a single "key" ratio for failure prediction
- models which use several financial ratios in combination for failure prediction.

W.H. Beaver (1966), investigating firms' financial ratios over a five-year period, studied 70 companies that were still going concerns and 70 that had failed. He found that the evidence overwhelmingly suggested that there was a difference in the ratios of failed and non-failed firms.

He went on to consider whether any single financial ratio was a reliable predictor of business failure, and found that the most reliable indicator was a ratio with cash flow, or perhaps profit, above the line and assets or liabilities below the line. He concluded that the ratio of cash flow to total debt was the best predictor of failure.

Single ratio analysis to predict corporate failure has been found, with experience, to be inadequate and unreliable, although much attention has been focused in recent years on the interest cover ratio. Some researchers have developed prediction models that identify and use a small number of key ratios, which can be combined into an aggregate "score" or financial health rating.

Z Scores

The concept of a Z score has been developed by Professor Redward Altman in the US, and (separately) by other researchers such as Professor Richard Taffler in the UK. A Z score is a figure (a "score") which can be calculated from a small number of financial ratios. Most of the data to calculate the ratios can be obtained from the published accounts of a company or group of companies and used to assess its financial health.

Z score models are constructed by analyzing a large number of financial ratios for a sample of "healthy" companies and a sample of "failed" companies. Statistical analysis (multiple discriminate analysis) is then used:

- to identify a small number of key ratios which can be relied on to distinguish healthy from failed companies, and
- to calculate coefficients or values for each ratio to build up a Z score model.

A Z score formula is constructed as follows:

$$Z \text{ score} = C_1 R_1 + C_2 R_2 + C_3 R_3 + \ldots + C_n R_n$$

Where:

- R_1 R_2 R_3 . . . R_n are the key ratios identified, and there are $_n$ key ratios
- C_1 C_2 C_3 . . . C_n are corresponding coefficients or values to apply to each ratio

A high Z score indicates "health" and a low Z score indicates "potential failure".

Professor Altman (1968) analyzed 22 accounting and non-accounting "variables" for a selection of failed and non-failed firms in the US and from these, five key indicators emerged. These five indicators were then used to derive a Z score. Firms with a Z score above a certain level could be classified as financially sound, and firms with a Z score below a certain level could be categorized as potential failures. Altman also identified a "grey area" or range of Z scores in between the non-fail and failure categories in which eventual failure or non-failure was uncertain.

The Altman Z score model emerged as:

$$Z = 0.012X_1 + 0.014X_2 + 0.033X_3 + 0.006X_4 + 0.0099X_5$$

Where:

- $X_1 =$ working capital/total assets ratio
- $X_2 =$ retained earnings/total assets ratio
- $X_3 =$ earnings before interest and tax/total assets ratio
- $X_4 =$ market value of equity/book value of total debt ratio (i.e. a form of leverage)
- $X_5 =$ sales/total assets

In Altman's model, a Z score of above 2.99 indicated non-failure, and a Z score below 1.81 indicated potential failure. (In other models developed since, a Z score of below zero indicates financial difficulties.)

Altman's sample size was small and related to US firms. Subsequent research based on the similar principle of identifying a Z score predictor of business failure has produced different prediction models, using a variety of financial ratios and different Z score values as predictors of failure. It could be argued, for example, that Z score models appropriate for conditions in the US are different from those companies in other countries. Similarly, different Z score models could be appropriate for companies in different industries.

Example
This example shows how the Altman model may not necessarily be appropriate

for all countries. In this example the financial statements are based on those of a small quoted company in the UK prior to its eventual collapse. At the time these financial statements were produced, the market value of the company's equity had fallen to about £4 million.

It is interesting to see what its Z score was, using the Altman model.

		Year 2
		£000
Working capital		1,146
Total assets	(3,782 + 23,020)	26,802
Retained earnings (no dividends declared)		(14,240)
Earnings (before interest and tax)	(4,983) + 955	(4,028)
Market value		4,000
Book value of total debt	(21,874 + 2,041)	23,915
Sales		60,812

The value of each ratio in the Z score model is therefore as follows:

- $X_1 =$ $1,146 \div 26,802$ $=$ 0.043
- $X_2 =$ $(14,240) \div 26,802$ $=$ -0.531
- $X_3 =$ $(4,028) \div 26,802$ $=$ -0.150
- $X_4 =$ $4,000 \div 23,915$ $=$ 0.167
- $X_5 =$ $60,812 \div 26,802$ $=$ 2.269

The Z score of the company is as follows:

$$Z \text{ score} = (0.012)\,(0.043) + (0.014)\,(-0.531) + (0.033)\,(-0.150) + (0.006)$$
$$(0.167) + (0.0099)\,(2.269)$$
$$= \quad 0.001 - 0.007 - 0.005 + 0.001 + 0.022$$
$$= \quad 0.012$$

Analysis
Using Altman's model for a UK company in the construction and property industries is not wholly reliable, but the very low Z score of 0.012 is well below Altman's cut-off score of 1.81. The company would have been classified as a potential failure – in the event, an accurate prediction.

Professor Taffler has developed a Z score equation in the UK based on just four key ratios:

Ratio	Approx. weighting for quoted industrial companies	Analyzes
Profit before tax ÷ average current liabilities	53%	Profitability
Current assets ÷ total liabilities	13%	Working capital
Current liabilities ÷ total assets	18%	Financial risk
No credit interval (NCI)	16%	Liquidity

The NCI is the number of days a company can finance its operations from its immediate assets if it cannot guarantee any more revenue.

In Taffler's model, a Z score below 0 is a sign of potential difficulties, but details of the coefficients applied to each ratio are not available.

Professor Taffler has further extended the use of his model, from the calculation of a Z score (to identify companies that show characteristics of potential failure) to:

- risk rating, indicating the degree of risk on a scale of 1 to 5 of the company failing in the near future.
- comparisons with other similar companies (e.g. quoted industrial companies, unquoted industrial companies) and measuring the percentage of companies performing worse in the year in question.

The Value of Z Scores

A current view of the link between financial ratios and business failure is that certain financial ratios for firms which fail can be seen in retrospect to have deteriorated significantly prior to failure, and to be worse than the ratios of non-failed firms. Financial ratios can be used in retrospect to suggest why a firm has failed. However, no fully accepted model for *predicting* future business failures has yet been established even though some form of Z score analysis would appear to hold promise.

A Scores

A problem with Z scores is that the ratios are calculated with figures from a company's published accounts, but a company slipping into financial difficulties is more likely to adopt "creative accounting" techniques to improve the look of its statement of consolidated income (P&L in the UK) and balance sheet. When this happens, Z scores could fail to reflect the seriousness of the company's difficulties.

For this reason, John Argenti ("Corporate Collapse" 1976) developed an alternative approach to predicting corporate failure, based on more subjective judgements, to produce an A score.

Argenti argued that poor management causes companies to fail. Poor management has several manifestations, such as the combining of the roles of CEO and chairman in one person. The consequences of poor management include a deficient system of accounting and failure by the company to respond to change.

He also concluded from his research that poor management will make at least one of three other mistakes:

- They will overtrade
- They will launch a big project that goes wrong
- They will allow financial leverage to rise to a dangerously high level

Certain symptoms of deterioration will appear.

- Financial ratios will deteriorate
- Management will start to use creative accounting methods to present a better picture of results
- Various non-financial indicators will show deterioration
- Finally, the company will enter a "characteristic period" of (terminal) decline in its last few months

To construct an A score, Argenti took each of these management defects, mistakes and symptoms of failure and gave it a maximum score. Individual companies would be tested for each symptom, and given a score accordingly. An A score in excess of 25 out of 100 is an indication of potential difficulties.

Calculation of A Score

Defects	Maximum marks awarded
1. Autocrat at top	8
2. Chairman and chief executive = same person	4
3. Passive board	2
4. Unbalanced board	2
5. Weak finance director	2
6. Insufficient management	1
7. No budgetary control	3
8. No cash flow planning or reporting	3
9. No costing system	3
10. Slow response to changes in products or markets	<u>15</u>
Total	<u>43</u>
Pass Mark	10

Mistakes	
11. High gearing	15
12. Overtrading	15
13. Big project	<u>15</u>
Total	<u>45</u>
Pass Mark	15

Symptoms	
14. Financial signs of deterioration	4
15. Creative accounting	4
16. Non-financial signs of deterioration	3
17. Terminal signs	<u>1</u>
Total	<u>12</u>
Pass Mark	0
Total Possible Score	<u>100</u>
Pass Score	25
	(or less)

Summary

Z scores were devised to overcome two problems with ratio analysis. Analyzing 20 or 30 different ratios might not provide a clear picture of a company's financial position or creditworthiness. Some ratios might suggest financial strength whilst others suggest weakness. In ratio analysis, there is no single ratio with a single "minimum acceptable level" that can be used to identify companies in trouble. There are few, if any, unambiguous warning levels.

Z scores are less ambiguous, and provide an assessment of a company's financial position in a single figure. Credit analysts, particularly in banks, have used Z score analysis, and might still continue to do so. Opinion about the value of Z scores amongst practitioners is likely to vary over time and with experience. The concept of Z scores, however, remains an attractive one.

Glossary

A-score model
A small number of key ratios which, taken together, could be used as an indicator of the risk of business failure. It takes into consideration non-financial as well as financial factors in company failures. Companies are given a score for each key defect. The total of its score for each defect is its score. An A score above a certain level is an indication of a high risk of failure. This is an alternative to a Z-score model.

Accounting standards
These impose more specific rules for accounting on a company than are required by company law but still leave room for variation and judgment in accounts preparation.

The international body for setting accounting standards is the International Accounting Standards Board (IASB). All major countries adopt these accounting standards so there is a degree of uniformity around the world.

Asset turnover
Is a ratio focusing on the volume of sales achieved by the business. It measures the amount of sales turnover per $1 of assets employed. It is significant for profitability.

Auditors report
The auditor's report simply represents their opinion that the accounts give a true and fair view of the companyís financial affairs in accordance with company legislation.

Business risk
This arises from the possibility that a fall in the company's sales turnover or profit margins could occur as a consequence of changes in its business environment (new competition, technological change etc). It is longer term risk. One technique for assessing business risk is SWOT analysis (see below)

Cash flow analysis

This focuses on a company's ability to generate cash to pay off its loans and other debts.

Cash flow ratios

Cash flow ratios should be analyzed by looking at trends in the ratios over time, by making comparisons with the ratios of other companies and, occasionally, by judging a ratio for the company against a maximum or minimum sales ratio.

Chairman's report

This is normally released with the annual report and will comment on the group's activities, particularly future ones.

Competitive advantage

Competitive advantage is anything which gives one organization an edge over its rivals in the products it sells or the services it offers. It is a key factor for longer-term prosperity and survival.

Consolidated accounts

These are accounts for all companies within a group, of which the public company is the parent company (holding company). But a group of companies is not a legal entity. Consolidated accounts are only of value when credit is being granted to the parent company, or the parent company is providing a guarantee for repayment of credit by a subsidiary.

Creative accounting

This arises from the variety of alternative accounting policies that companies are permitted to use. The need for judgment also gives scope for adjustments to the figures.

Credit analysis

This is a systematic process for assessing and evaluating credit risk.

Credit analyst

This is someone who assesses the creditworthiness of individual corporate customers. He/she should gather information about the industry within which the company operates. An objective assessment should be made of the company's senior management. The analyst should look for expertize and experience, and for stability or continuity in the management team. When the roles of chairman and chief executive are combined, credit risk can depend on the character and management style of the individual.

Credit scoring
Looks at financial ratios to assess a company's creditworthiness.

Creditworthiness
A company's creditworthiness for longer-term borrowing will depend on the likely profits from its capital spending projects, and the expected speed of payback.

Current ratio
This compares the total value of current assets with the amount of current liabilities. In most companies (but not all) fewer current assets than short-term liabilities would indicate illiquidity.

Debt ratio
This compares the total amount of a company's debts (ie all its creditors) with the total value of its assets.

Depreciation
Depreciation can be defined as a measure of the wearing out, consumption or other loss of value of a fixed asset, whether arising from use, the passing of time or obsolescence through technological or market changes. Depreciation of fixed assets is a charge against profits. Depreciation charges can vary on similar fixed assets according to the company's views about their expected useful life, their estimated residual value and the preferred method of depreciation.

Discretionary cash flows
These are cash receipts or payments that are not essential and not connected directly with the trading operations. They include the purchase and sale of fixed asset and dividend payments.

Financial cash flows
These are cash receipts and payments from changes in long-term capital, such as new loans or cash from the issue of new shares.

Financial ratios
These are commonly used in assessing a company's creditworthiness. Each ratio has a specific purpose and focuses on a particular aspect of a company's financial position. Ratios and percentages compare the size of one item with

another. They are used in financial analysis to give meaning and significance to numbers that might otherwise not be apparent.

Financial reports/statements
Financial reports or statements from a company are a key source of credit risk information. They give information about revenues, costs and profits, cash flows, assets and liabilities. The most commonly-used source of financial information about a company is its annual report and account. This document will be at least several months out of date. The accounts of public companies are almost invariably consolidated accounts for a group, of which the public company is the parent company (holding company).

Financial risk
This refers to the possibility that a company will be unable to repay its debts in full and on time. It is commonly measured by its leverage ratio. This compares the size of the company's interest-bearing debts with the amount of stockholder funds. A company's financial risk increases as its leverage ratio rises.

Goodwill
Goodwill on acquisition is the difference between the purchase of the acquired subsidiary and the fair value of the assets acquired. The most common way to account for goodwill is to write off goodwill against reserves. This cost of goodwill does not then have to be amortised (depreciated) as a charge against profits in future years.

Gross profit
Is the values of sales minus the cost of sales

Income statement
The income statement (or profit or loss account in the UK) should disclose any exceptional or extraordinary items. These could have increase or reduce profits significantly.

Interest cover
This covers the company's interest charges with the amount of profits available to pay the interest. A fall in the profit/interest charges ratio could be an indication of a deteriorating financial position.

Internal financing ratio
This measures the proportion of capital expenditures that have been paid out

of available operational cash flows.

The International Accounting Standards Board (IASB)
This body sets accounting standards around the world.

Liquidity
This is the ability to convert assets into cash or ready access to cash. Liquidity can be measured by comparing the value of a company's liquid assets with the amount of short-term liabilities.

Liquid assets
These are cash or current assets that will be soon be converted into a cash receipt.

Management accounts
These are budgets and forecasts prepared for the company for internal management purposes. They are not always available to the credit analyst. Forecasts may also be over-optimistic and unreliable.

Net cash flow
This is the total change in a company's cash balances over a period of time.

No Credit Interval (NCI)
This is another measure of liquidity. On the assumption that the company were to stop trading immediately, it is the estimate of the number of days the company could continue to pay for its operating expenses before running out of cash.

Operational cash flow
This is the actual net receipts (or net outlays) of cash over a period of time from trading operations.

Overtrading
Companies that expand too quickly, financed by insufficient long-term capital, are overtrading.

Priority cash flows
These are cash payments for non-trading items that a company must make to avoid financial collapse. They include interest and tax payments.

Product differentiation

A differentiation strategy seeks to raise the quality of the product and sell it at a higher price. It is one way of achieving a competitive edge

Profitability analysis

Three ratios are used for assessing profitability: return on capital employed; profit margin; and asset turnover.

Profit margin

Is the size of a company's profit in relation to its sales turnover and it is usually expressed as a percentage figure. It can be measured as a gross margin or a net profit margin can be described as either high margin or low margin. Falling margins result in lower profits.

Quick ratio (or acid test ratio)

This compares the value of a companies 'quick' assets (i.e. current assets except for stocks) with the amount of its current liabilities. An excess of current liabilities over quick assets could suggest inadequate liquidity.

Return on capital employed (or return on assets)

It is the profit margin multiplied by the asset turnover. A high return is desirable.

Return on equity

This can be regarded as the product of its business risk (profit margins and asset turnover) and its financial risk.

SWOT analysis

This is a technique for assessing business risk. This is a tabulation of the company's strengths, weaknesses and opportunities and threats.

Working capital

This is a company's investment in its current assets. A useful definition of working capital is stocks plus debtors minus short-term creditors.
The amount of working capital that a business needs fluctuates continually, and can charge by large amounts over time. The need for working capital is linked to the trading and cash cycles.

Z-score models

These identify a small number of key financial ratios which, taken together, could be used as an indicator of the risk of business failure. Each Z-score model has its own key ratios. Different Z-score models are required for companies in different industries and countries.

Index